This book will encourage you to pave your own path, be bold, and find personal freedom outside societal stereotypes.

—Virginia Novak, BSN, Clinical Research

For those of us seeking answers on this journey through life, **Trust Your Animal Instincts** *helps us find the courage to let go of the "shoulds" permeating our lives and to listen to the universal source at the center of us all.*

— Bo Bass, President, Beaux Land Development Services

A well-written story of self-exploration that led Tabitha to start a new and more fulfilling life. She uses her excellent storytelling skills to share the wisdom she gained on her journey and tops it off with guides for you to do your own journeys without having to leave the house. A worthwhile read.

— Victoria E. Slater, RN, PhD, AHN-BC, CHTP/I

Trust Your Animal Instincts *is an inspiring story that I believe will help people by teaching them how to let go, develop faith in themselves, and to embrace constant change.*

— C. McDonald, Department of Defense Program Manager

An animal's role as a spiritual messenger is often overlooked. Reading this book will provide insight as to how this awareness may manifest in your life. After enjoying this book, you will look at your interactions with people, events, pets and other animals around you in a totally different and powerful light.

— K'Leetha Gilbert, Science Instructor, Davidson County–Metro Nashville Schools

Trust Your Animal Instincts *is a testament that we can overcome those inner barriers and demons entrenched in our psyche through resilience, nurture, love, and self-reflection. Tabitha shows us that opening oneself up to the child-like qualities of boundless curiosity, energy, and wonder can help us navigate through life's clutter and noise to experience the mystical world of healing and inspiration.*

— John Kim, EdD, MPH, University of Kentucky, College of Medicine

D0188134

TRUST
YOUR
ANIMAL
INSTINCTS

Recharge Your Life & Ignite Your Power

TRUST YOUR ANIMAL INSTINCTS

TABITHA A. SCOTT

powering
POTENTIAL

POWERING POTENTIAL MEDIA

p⏻wering POTENTIAL

Published by Powering Potential Media

ISBN (paperback): 978-1-7354940-0-5
ISBN (e-book): 978-1-7354940-1-2

Edited by Lauren Helmer, LaurenHelmerCreative.com
Cover and interior design by Christy Collins, Constellation Book Services
Author photograph by Deb Loveland

Printed in the United States of America

Contents

Acknowledgments

Writing a book is more difficult than I ever imagined and could not have been done without the loving support of my family and friends. First, thanks to Bobby and Edwanna Scott for giving me a firm foundation in faith, optimism, and creativity. And to my sons, Trent and Ethan, who are my biggest supporters and sources of inspiration. Thanks also to my sister for providing a good example of equal parts toughness and love.

Thanks to K'Leetha Gilbert for introducing me to energy healing and encouraging heart-based thinking, to James Haussermann for reminding me it's OK for adults to take time for childlike adventures, and to J.B. Langston for helping me refine the focus for this first book, which allowed me to finish it. A great deal of gratitude goes to editor and contributor Lauren Helmer. Her insights as a working mom and talented, caring professional helped me undertake what seemed like an impossible task of writing a book on nights, holidays, and weekends. Also, I appreciate Martha Bullen's wisdom, guidance, and "hand-holding" to navigate the complex process of publishing.

The look and feel of this book are thanks to a seasoned crew of brilliant artists. Christy Collins worked her magic and creativity to create the perfect vibe for this book cover and its interior design. At the last minute, we decided to use real photos from the trip, as well as personally created artwork. Experienced artist Charlotte Cash provided illustrations within just a few days' notice. Dennis Hogan, an award-winning designer, was responsible for the Should Monster and Inner Owl logos as well as other design work. And, thanks to artist Ethan Crawford for advising on concepts and allowing me to use his art.

My heartfelt gratitude to friends who provided valuable feedback and guidance along the way. Your personal support and input on the science, medical references, writing, and personal stories proved I have dear friends who have my back as I captured life excerpts and penned original ideas: Bo Bass, Stacy Clayton, Andrew Diamond, Lily Hansen, Dustin Helmer, John Kim, Stephen Kulinski, Richard Lucy, Steven McDonald, Chris Mead, Michael Modrak, Rob Nowak, Shiro Onedera, Bill Owen, Dave Pelton, Neil Rodgers, Becky Hale Russell, Vicki Slater, Chad Smith, Randy Stacy, Jeff Stough, and Stephen Worthy.

Thanks to my career mentors, Dana Bowers, Jim Evans, Jim Fugitte, and Chris Williams. Their guidance in business, support through continued education, trust with the companies they led, and ongoing encouragement shaped my success and increased my confidence to take big risks.

Introduction

*Security is mostly a superstition. It does not exist in nature,
nor do the children of men as a whole experience it. Avoiding
danger is no safer in the long run than outright exposure.
Life is either a daring adventure or nothing.*

— HELEN KELLER

He and his troop could attack in a heartbeat—how many were hiding in this thick canopy? I was 9 degrees north of the heat-scorched equator in Costa Rica, isolated and afraid. Samson, the alpha howler monkey I encountered last week, stared down at me from a jungle branch just 6 feet away. Howlers are among the largest monkeys in the Western Hemisphere and are named for their thunderous roars that are heard up to 3 miles away. Known to be cranky towards humans and prone to throwing poo at unwelcome guests, these weren't the cute little "organ grinder" monkeys seen at the circus.

My water supply was depleted, I was lightheaded from dehydration and heat, and the situation was imminently perilous. I decided to focus on making it back safely to the trailhead before the sun sank further—once it set for the day, the canopy ceiling would shield all means of natural navigation. I slowed from running to slowly walking to conserve energy while panic crept up the path behind me. The bad thing about walking at a slow pace in the jungle is you not only hear the lizards and snakes whooshing away from the trail, sometimes you can feel them beneath your soles.

My heart was a bass drum pounding louder with each step as the thought crossed my mind, *What will become of me if I don't find my way out of this jungle?* Clarity arose as I connected those experiences in the wild with my experiences navigating our fast-paced, worrisome world back home. Unpredictability lurked on all sides, survival hummed beneath every little decision, time shape-shifted, and my personal direction seemed unclear. The solution, tuning in to my animal instinct, was always there; I just hadn't stopped running long enough to hear it.

As I write this, the jungle that is our world and its technologies is endlessly and exponentially evolving—it feels like running a race with no finish line, yet to compete, you must keep getting faster. And with the coronavirus pandemic of 2020, the world we inhabit is not only changing fast, but it morphed into an entirely new and uncharted terrain … unrecognizable, even. City streets, once bustling, became empty except for the trees, birds, and animals. Economic conditions are spiraling out of control, and we're witnessing fear, apprehension, and death on a scale most of us have never seen. The streets are filling up again, but with protesters alongside pedestrians, as injustice, opposing political views, and harmful bias fuel further uncertainty.

Even before the world was forced into temporary isolation, the internet's Wild West rules, anonymity for all, constant barrage of ads, and the 24-hour emails and news cycles all provided distractions that polarized, alienated, and reshaped the ways we think and interact. There are so many inputs to filter, so much change to interpret, and so little time to react. The pace of change itself continues to multiply, feeding an addiction to our mobile devices, tablets, and screens just so we can feel like we're keeping up or at least feeling connected.

As an executive and a Southern mom, I've run with and from the frenetic pace myself. During my most stressful years, I ran both literally and figuratively, completing six marathons in about 18 months while also fleeing from the confines of social judgment, toxic relationships, incurable family illnesses, a challenging job, and a political landscape to which I could no longer relate.

Introduction

I fled the busyness of the city and lived for nearly three months in the Costa Rican jungle—with no convenient phone service, television, radio, or other means of connectivity. So many questions were running through my mind ... *How do we find and maintain peace and happiness amidst the encircling storm of uncertainty? Is it possible to connect directly to the spirit realm without being some sort of guru? Where is that joy I had as a kid, and can it set me free from the pressures of the modern world, allowing me to feel love again?*

What I learned while balancing at the edge of a "fast-forward" civilization was that no matter how far or how fast I ran, the feeling of true freedom from burnout, stress, and anxiety was achieved most quickly by selecting "pause." I discovered how to reconnect to that innate source of life-giving energy, that deep-seated wisdom within, and I listened to it. I found a way to identify and shed the harmful pressures we put on ourselves. And I uncovered how to survive the burnout that comes from trying to keep pace with ever-changing technology and social uncertainty.

From deep within the Costa Rican jungle, my own intuition emerged. And something in me felt like a carefree kid again with unbridled, authentic joy. Some call it a "still, small voice," but to me it was like reconnecting directly with the higher Spirit using my own personal speed-dial number, allowing me to shed my worries.

What did freedom from worry feel like? It is an endless fountain of happy-belly energy. It's the kind of energy we feel before blowing out the candles on a birthday cake, the excitement of hanging out with that friend who makes us laugh so hard we lose track of time, and the ever-present joy of connectedness that comes naturally from within us. We have the power to create or destroy that feeling at any time, to hold close to or let go of negativity, and to believe in or break down ourselves—and others.

And while uncertainty may lurk in our modern world, bravery and kindness are emerging in inspiring new ways. Beautiful creativity and celebrations of humanity are happening through virtual dance parties, trivia games, and dinners on Zoom; children are taking art classes and guitar lessons through online portals; and people across the globe are working and attending school from their devices. Striving to make good come out of tough times, we cling to patience and love—staying safely distanced, cultivating new hobbies, banging pots from balconies, and challenging old ways of thinking. Regardless of which jungle we are in, it can be frightening, rejecting, and isolating, and, at the same time, alluring, adventurous, and fascinating.

It took years of reflection, research, study, and practice since living through my jungle catharsis to articulate them in a meaningful way. We are each born into different geographies, traditions, and beliefs that shape our paradigms and impact our lives. Our outward appearances, our education, and our talents are all unique. We strive, discover, compete, and seek, joining with or dividing ourselves from others along the way. We look outward, taking cues from society about how we "should" look, what roles we "should" adopt, and how we "should" define success.

But what if I told you there is no difference between us? The things that outwardly divide us disappear when we look inward, because we're all made of the exact same energy. The same energy that formed the universe, that is the source of all major world religions, and that flows freely and abundantly through each of us. We each grow into different beliefs, paradigms, and levels of success, but we are all born as "energists"—made of the same divine, perfect, and renewable resource.

What has been spiritually taught since the dawn of mankind is now confirmed by quantum and physical science. Upon embracing this truth, and as a long-time leader in the energy sector, I was astounded how the sources, characteristics, and science of electricity drive all of our interactions. Energy itself is the lifeblood of all living things, and we can all tap into it to reconnect.

It doesn't take a trip to the jungle to reconnect through your own intuition. All you need is belief in the Spirit, belief in yourself, and belief in love. In this book, I share my journey of discovering—or rediscovering—and trusting my own animal instincts. And, I've shared the steps taken so that you, too, may recharge your life and ignite your own power.

PART 1

From Spark Plug to Burnout

Striking Imbalance

CHAPTER 1

Static Electricity

Static Electricity: Static electricity is an imbalance of charges. It is created when two objects that don't naturally conduct electricity are rubbed together. Huge static sparks can ignite during storms to produce dangerous lightning, with striking temperatures of up to 50,000 degrees Fahrenheit.

I'm a recovering skeptic. I was addicted to being logical, accommodating, professional, and rational. I avoided uncomfy things like emotions, spirituality, and even love itself. But I'm on the road to recovery now, thanks to the realization that life is not about choosing sides: being logical *or* intuitive, rational *or* emotional, scientific *or* spiritual. Instead, it's about having the freedom to embrace all of those qualities at the same time. You see, the truth that set me free was the understanding that reality itself is the intersection where quantum science meets spirituality. My existence had been an ongoing event defined for myself in every moment; I just didn't know it yet.

Everything was interwoven, but how? I got caught up in the frenetic search to find answers, to seek clarity, and to pursue the truth beyond the world's definition of how things should be. They told me the perfect resumé boasts a strong action verb at the beginning of each line: driving, leading, developing. So, I spent decades building one that could compete with the best. They said it was most important to demonstrate what you do, so I tried to please everyone—family, friends, colleagues, and churchgoers.

I didn't realize that true power came instead from who you are and that it's born from those actions that could be considered passive, like listening, feeling, and loving. There was so much pressure about the choices I'd made in the past and which ones I would choose next. The focus was on selecting the "right" path instead of comprehending that all paths offered equal opportunity to invent, then reinvent, my real-time, personal definition of "success."

Have you ever felt buried under the weight of endless expectations, knowing that there was no way you could meet them all? Do you feel frustrated or guilty for not spending enough time with family and friends, or working, or doing something that feels good for yourself? Does it ever seem like no matter how much you achieve, that something is still missing? Are there certain people in your life that just thinking about them makes you feel off balance? I thought feeling "good" or "bad" was tied to accomplishments, so I used to spend a lot of time trying to live up to the world's expectations.

These refrains kept running on repeat in my mind: *You should be a good girl. Follow tradition and don't ask too many questions along the way. Submit to your husband, obey the religious rules defined thousands of years ago, and by all means do it with grace, humility, and beauty. Strive to be appropriate, acceptable, agreeable, and normal. Keep up with the latest at the kids' schools, in the neighborhood, with the faith community, and you really should wear a more attractive, ladylike pair of heels instead of those comfy shoes—for goodness' sake, it's important to look fashionable (bless your heart).*

You should be a powerful leader. You made it to CEO by age 30, then a senior executive at two global companies during the next decade, so we're expecting more from you. We're counting on you to suck it up; never let them see your weaknesses; outperform, inspire, compete, be strong, and lead. Be that mentor for other women who want success, push the boundaries, drive the business forward, and ditch your twangy Southern accent—it doesn't serve you in the boardroom or behind the podium. Keep up with the latest in economic trends, the energy sector, and global trade policies. And for God's sake, polish those damn shoes before you return to the Pentagon—you're working with top brass now, and it's important to look the part.

The clashing worlds of a Southern, conservative mom and a hard-charging, progressive executive made it feel impossible to keep everyone happy, including myself. No matter which shoes I was wearing at the time, nothing seemed to fit expectations. It was like decades of Chinese water torture. You know, when a captive is forced to endure a slow, steady drip ... drip ... drip ... of water. At first, it seems like nothing. It's only one tiny droplet of water at a time, after all. But, over time, the skin wears thin and each subsequent drop feels heavier than the last, eventually creating unbearable pain. Decades of "shoulds" from society, colleagues, family, friends, and myself that I could no longer outrun felt like a thousand baby birds hungrily pecking at me, each one patiently waiting its turn to take a tiny piece of my potential, then politely "should-ing" on me before flying back to its nest.

It was like running a marathon and getting to the end, then the finish line was moved further away. *Just a little farther*, I would think. *Hang in there. You're almost there!* I wondered, *Where is "there," that proverbial finish line? And does anyone ever actually arrive?*

Amidst the increasing fatigue, I unexpectedly had to deal with a cancer scare. A quick search on WebMD to understand more about my situation and the decisions at hand revealed a study of the impact stress had on women's health. It concluded that those under significant stress had twice the risk of developing breast cancer as women who managed to stay calm. *No surprise there*, I thought. Grateful for the gift of early detection, I called my insurance company to be sure everything would be covered, then informed the surgeon I was ready to go ahead: "Just take what you need to remove the risk."

It was as if one day I awoke to the realization that all of a sudden, the kids had grown and gone, my 21-year marriage was over, my career had been based on implementing ideas nobody seemed to care about, and the combined stress was starting to impact my health. There was no triumphant finish to this race. My life had become like a fake smile in a selfie. Everyone could see me beaming in the post, but the joy inside had grown tired and despondent.

How had I gotten here—and where the hell was I supposed to go next?

Freedom

CHAPTER 2

From the Farm to the Big City

Horse: The horse symbolizes personal drive, passion, and appetite for freedom. Horses also represent the balance between instinctive and tamed parts of our personality.

Growing up as a tomboy in small-town Kentucky, I was comfortable holding my own with the guys. My best friends were often boys because we played sports, rode horses, drove motorcycles, and enjoyed other adventures that weren't considered girly activities in those days. My rough-and-tumble spirit often clashed with my father's stern discipline to create an emotional landscape at home that was tricky terrain. Dad was a popular educator, a coach, a church leader, a seasoned fisherman, and was impossible to outshoot. He was also known in the community for his quick-witted comedy and at home for his quick temper. I learned at an early age to shoot a gun, drive a tractor, stay inside the lines, anticipate escalations, and most importantly, to use my own sense of humor to stay in his good graces.

While I looked like Dad and shared his inability to sit still, Mom provided a good contrast with her patient, traditional, creative, and loving manner. Until I was a mother myself, I had little appreciation for how she managed to juggle a career in education, have home-cooked meals on the table each night, and run us to endless lessons, sports practices, and activities. She taught me a love for all creatures and that they each had a valuable purpose in God's plan. Every summer it was our tradition to find a milkweed plant in the field with a striped caterpillar on it. We would bring it inside and watch the caterpillar pupate into a self-made chrysalis. In a few weeks, it would emerge into a beautiful monarch butterfly. Insects, spiders, snakes, puppies, cows, birds, mice, and everything else—they were meant to be respected because they all had interesting attributes and important purposes.

Mom made learning feel like a fun game. Like when we went shopping together at the local grocery, the IGA store, she would buy me an ICEE if I could add up the items we put into the cart in my head and it matched the charges that rang up on the cash register upon checkout. I had no idea I was computing mathematics, only that if I got it right, I would get to choose either a cherry- or cola-flavored frozen drink at the end.

As a young girl, I imagined myself a tough superhero who could break free from the endless list of rules while fighting imaginary battles alongside my animal friends. Sometimes our spotted Dalmatian dog, Peppi, was a regal steed pulling my homemade chariot from the burning ruins. Other times, my horse, Betty, was the best means of transportation into the unknown wilderness, while my sister's striped orange cat, Dusty, perched behind the saddle, meowing with encouragement the whole way. These animals were trusted confidants that protected me from both fact and fiction. I often spent the days outdoors, fully absorbed in these adventures until summoned in for the night. An unquenchable, infectious energy always propelled me onward, despite—or *in spite of*—any odds that might have been stacked against me. I would compete in almost any sport or rebuild the chariot made out of old wheels from the garage a dozen times to keep improving it, to make it perfect. Having obstacles made me savor success even more because giving up or giving in would have meant losing the game.

Dad didn't believe in mistakes, only stupid decisions, so while normal kids were grounded or lectured for their poor choices, I had to write. I wrote thousands of sentences over the years. And my spelling, especially for words like *prudent, judgment,* and *responsible,* became flawless. While Dad didn't believe in mistakes, they materialized quite effortlessly for me. They were like tiny hidden land mines—risky little challenges too tempting to pass up, a forgotten chore, or perhaps pestering my older sister.

My sister was nearly two years older than me, always got straight As in school, and used to torture me by chasing me with terrifying things like ketchup and mayonnaise. Not to be outdone, I learned not only could I send her running, but the babysitter as well, with *equally* frightening things like a dead snake from the woods or a handmade slingshot. Since our parents didn't share my sense of fairness, I did the logical thing and stockpiled sentences on rainy days or when bored during class to get ahead of the punishment curve. *I will be more responsible. I will use more prudent judgment in the future. I will be more respectful to my sister.*

True enough, if a word had anything to do with improving behavior, I could most certainly spell it. Not to mention, I was winning the punishment game. Just as we were required to use proper grammar (which even included writing sentences if we said "ain't"), one of the nonnegotiable requirements as a child was attending church up to three times every week. My grandma had an old piano, so when I visited, I played little songs from church, beginning around age 4. I couldn't read the notes in the hymnal, but I would "hear" a hymn a certain way in my mind, and somehow those vibrations would be transferred onto the keys.

It felt as if the song was flowing from my heart. The Bible calls this guidance the "Holy Spirit," and it was my first memory of feeling a power provide something greater than what I had the ability to do on my own. It was purely intuition-based. My mind was somewhere else, and if I stopped to think about where to place my hands, it would throw off that connection, resulting in mistakes. Anyone witnessing great jazz musicians knows that overthinking it kills the power and beauty of intuitive improvisation.

This ability did not make logical sense, but it brought me—and hopefully others—a feeling of freedom and joy. From what must have been around the age of 8, I began playing the piano for special music performances at church. By age 10, I also accompanied our school choral festivals on occasion. Sometimes a rendition would evoke tears and other times clapping along. I loved building to fast, foot-stomping, Southern Gospel-style endings, imagining we could just get wound up enough to step right on through the Pearly Gates of Heaven ourselves. It taught me the crescendo of joy that arose from sharing my love with others and how the same arrangement could touch different people in different ways.

I also taught myself to play simple duets with my fingers and toes, but was sternly forbidden to perform them at church. Also banned was chewing bubble gum in public, because it was unladylike, so I learned some incredible gum-hiding techniques over the years. Childhood was a constant ebb and flow between conformity and creativity. Sometimes the outcomes were breakthroughs and other times they were disasters. In hindsight, perhaps the ban on gum was more about protecting my hair than appearing proper. As a youngster, my floppy crop of curls was snipped short on more than one occasion in the aftermath of an overzealous bubble-gum-blowing contest gone wrong.

Growing up on a small farm, we worked hard. It was simple: If we wanted something, we worked odd jobs to raise our own money and buy it. Each achievement came with its own responsibilities. The chickens and ducks were to be secured behind doors overnight. Forgetting to do so left them vulnerable to the whims of hungry weasels and foxes. The horses had to be groomed, fed, and watered; their stalls had to be mucked; and they must be locked into their stalls at night. (If they weren't, the "I will be more responsible" sentences would be penned by yours truly.)

There was nothing as powerful as the feeling of riding my horse across the field. Sometimes I took time to saddle her up and take along the cat, but I usually just hopped on with bare feet and a bridle and took off. The feeling transcended time—it made me forget about everything except the wind on my face and the ground rushing by beneath us. Like skipping my little fingers across the piano keys, riding Betty gave me a powerful feeling of complete control and a thrilling sense of wild freedom.

While trusting people didn't always come naturally to me because their motives often seemed awry, I had absolute trust in my horse's instincts of when to run through or jump over an obstacle. I relished both the risk and safety of sitting high above the ground. And we were always pushing the boundaries, sneaking beyond the barbed-wire fence on the back side of our 20-acre farm. Wandering down abandoned railroad tracks, into streams, over fallen trees—there were seemingly endless quests to conquer. This was the second time I remember feeling an energy from within that I couldn't explain.

Horses are like dogs—they want to please us and provide great joy and companionship. Their care and feeding was well worth the effort. I remember one evening reaching into the large feed bin to get food for the horses and being greeted by an angry opossum wedged deep inside. I reasoned, *Dad always says snakes are more afraid of us than we are of them, so it's probably the same with 'possums.*

At the time, I had two horses, three chickens (which were taught to shake hands), a duck that walked sideways, a dog, two cats, and an older sister. But not a 'possum—yet. This was my chance to make a meaningful connection. Gently, I leaned in to negotiate with the little fella in hopes he would voluntarily climb out, or better yet, let me pet him. "Hey there little possy-poo, whatcha doin' in there?" He leapt from the bin and chased me halfway to the house before I outran him—spiny teeth bared and hissing louder than my terrified shrieks. *Note to self: He was not more afraid of me than I was of him. Second note to self: Wild 'possums don't make good pets.*

By any standard, I had an adventurous existence that ultimately equipped me for an accomplished career. But it took time and perspective to realize the importance of each contributing block in the foundation of success. Growing up with parents who were elementary educators, we had limited financial resources and little exposure to the world of business. City life was a big, exciting mystery to me. I remember asking our beloved rural public school advisor how to go about selecting a college and her response: "Well, honey, they're all just about the same. You did real well on your entrance exams, so just pick one."

I wanted to be a business executive, so I reckoned choosing a college in the largest city in Kentucky made sense. It never even occurred to me that it was possible to apply outside our state. That's the entire extent of planning that went into initiating my formal education. While my lack of exposure to the business world, country clubs, sororities, and connections initially put me behind others in the workplace, I had a deep sense of gratitude for the important privileges we did inherit: hard work, risk-taking, determination, resilience, and optimism. And, guess what? It worked out just fine. I'm eternally grateful for this path because having modest roots added to my complexity, relatability, and empathy—all strong traits that could not be purchased.

While finishing my degree in business finance, I worked at Capital Holding Corporation in the tech department. After that, some interesting roles followed: hotel manager, credit card analyst, and even tourism writer before eventually becoming CEO of a small, Kentucky-based electronic payments company by the age of 30. Like a character in one of my backyard adventures at home as a kid, I fearlessly knocked on countless doors at the Pentagon, eventually edging out corporate giants EDS and Bank of America for the largest contract of its kind in history to transfer monthly rent payments for a $20 billion government housing revitalization effort.

The life game continued after that as I launched into renewable energy and innovation, working first as senior VP for a global Sydney-based corporation, then as senior VP for a 200-year-old London-based infrastructure investments company. I use the term 'game' because I chose that field out of my love for the environment, not just to make a living, so it brought a great deal of satisfaction during the early years.

A large part of those roles was centered on the science of behavior change—influencing behaviors to adopt a new business model, to try a new technology, to use less energy, to take calculated risks. It seemed I should have been able to solve the world's energy problems and reduce pollution in one fell swoop. *Why not?* I eagerly scaled the corporate ladder for many years using the same zeal as climbing the giant trees in the fencerow as a child.

Each of us are born with varying privileges. For some of us, it takes time and perspective to recognize our unique backgrounds as positive influences that shape our personal power. For me, having a humble background served as fuel. It kept me focused on finding opportunities, proving execution, and thanking the people who gave me a chance. It also taught me to know when to put up a fight and when to walk away. I chose to compete for what I wanted in life, not to blame those with privileges for my lack thereof, always believing it possible to achieve my own American dream. Being raised on a rural farm also gave me an opportunity to grow my own strong friends and family network organically over the years.

The dream wasn't unique to me—anybody who believes in themselves and their dreams can do it. Asking for the promotions I wanted, rather than waiting for them to be granted, helped me move up the corporate ladder and achieve my goal of exploring the world. My career aligned with my passion, and I was grateful to travel—something I'd held as a dream as long as I could remember. I journeyed overseas to work in London, hike the Alps, convene in Jerusalem, dance in Barcelona, dive in Bahamian waters, and sail the Virgin Islands. Each experience held new discoveries and welcomed expansions of my Southern paradigms. This was the season of life I had toiled endlessly to achieve—an accomplished career, two independent sons, a home in the suburbs. It all seemed like the good life, at least from the outside looking in.

Bless Your Heart!

Southern Charm

CHAPTER 3

Getting "Should On"

*Burnout: [burn·out] n. 1. a fire that is totally destructive
of something 2. the breakdown of an electrical device due to
the heat created by the currents flowing through it*

That plucky childhood spark began to dull as life progressed with the pressures of college, marriage, career, children … Despite feeling burned out, work life was at least predictable. I studied the trends, understood the economics, worked hard, saw opportunities, and made things happen. My personal life, on the other hand, was an unbridled series of challenges. No matter how much effort I put into creating a perfect family life, it seemed fate simply chuckled at my efforts. Whether working at an office or from home, the mental, physical, and emotional requirements of moms and wives are vastly undervalued.

Even with more equality for gender roles in the workplace, women are still largely expected to manage the household, create the meals, handle the family's medical issues, support school and sports activities, *and* remain attractive for their spouse—oh, *and* bring home the bacon. Like most good Southern women, I did my best to graciously and gracefully deliver on all of the above without complaint. *What would the neighbors think if we bucked tradition?*

"Those poor kids … their mom is always working. She should be home more." "Do you think she knows her son was smoking pot the other day? She should know that." "Did you notice Tabitha is starting to get thick in the thighs? She should find her way back to the gym."

During the decades of having children and being dutifully married, I did my best to uphold the got-it-together executive and good Christian mom images. Challenges were dealt with swiftly and tucked away neatly to prevent signs of weakness. I had a job convincing people to change habits, and a home life accommodating a spouse who wanted me to be someone else. He wanted a Ree Drummond, aka "The Pioneer Woman," who stayed home on the farm where she happily cooked and cared for her brood. Instead, he got an ever-curious and progressive executive, a Liz Lemon from "30 Rock." We simply rushed into marriage within months to appease tradition, without giving long-term goals much of a thought. After all, we were both friendly people from good Christian families—what else mattered?

We encountered major road bumps when our two sons each faced serious medical challenges. Starting in middle school, my younger son, Ethan, had five surgeries to bind together overly flexible knees from a very rare condition. It was excruciating to watch a popular, outgoing, and athletic child shift from running around the neighborhood himself, to being wheelchair-bound, watching from the window as others played outside.

My eldest son, Trent, became temporarily incapacitated at age 16 with narcolepsy, an incurable autoimmune sleeping disorder. He couldn't function during classes, and we began what seemed like an unending quest to find answers, anything that could offer relief and hope. It gradually became clear that traditional medicine was not enough … but I kept searching.

I wanted to be the best employee, leader, spouse, and mom, yet constantly felt like I was failing. I was constantly allowing myself to be "should" on. The other executives in the office were men with wives who were full-time homemakers or schoolteachers (who were home when the children were on breaks). They nearly all had kids who were in private schools or were painstakingly homeschooled, and they had strong opinions about me allowing my kids to attend public schools. The other moms in our suburban neighborhood were mostly in traditional feminine roles, with few exceptions.

I have great admiration and respect for educators. The reality was that while I liked the idea of having more time with our kids, there was no way I could have held the attention of a classroom for an entire day, much less a school year. There were only two lessons I was capable of leading when volunteering at school—one was about the history of pumpkins and the other was about the history of money. Both lessons blatantly and unashamedly used bribery, either a tiny pumpkin or a dollar, to get the little munchkins to sit still for an hour.

Whether at home or at work, I was quite used to being an oddball. I experienced a constant conflict between craving to be liked and accepted and the yearning to fully blaze my own path.

- "You should be in the office as much as the male executives or else they'll think you're weak or not working as hard."

- "You should not travel so much for work. Your family will not get the attention they deserve."

- "You should be able to convince your husband to attend counseling or church and just work it out."

- "You should pray harder, longer, and with the right heart, then God will heal your sons."

- "You should attend the company's remote two-week training sessions, and you should relocate your family if you want to remain competitive in this industry."

- "You should be a stay-at-home mom or teacher if you have children. If you try to be an executive, your kids will surely suffer."

- "You should marry someone quickly, because you're damaging your son by being a single mom. There's something wrong with you to be in this position."

I was fatefully imprisoned by everyone else's "shoulds." To an extent, we all are. And the connectedness of social media—along with images of everyone else's picture-perfect lives—magnifies the toxicity of these "shoulds." I was first exposed to this concept in 2007 by Tracy Goss, the author of *The Last Word on Power*. She planted a seed that grew over time into a powerful shift in my own perception of how to separate what others think from my own opinions and how important it is to recognize the difference.

At some point during that growth, it occurred to me that accommodating these "shoulds" that didn't align with my own views had created an unhealthy addiction that manifested in unnecessary shame, isolation, and burnout. I discovered my personal definition of burnout: "the negative effects caused by doing things that consume, rather than recharge, our energetic balance." It was impossible to please everyone, even when I had the best of intentions, yet I found myself constantly accommodating others' needs and expectations. It took me nearly a decade of understanding this concept logically before I began executing it powerfully.

Over many years of sharing this idea with others through personal conversations and public speaking engagements, I realized I needed a way to make the "should" concept easier to recognize. My friends who are counselors or psychologists recommended that I use a common technique used to identify triggers for addiction or anxiety by giving these pressures or negative feelings a name. Naming the occurrences gives us a sense of power over them, depersonalizes them, and makes them easier to ignore, avoid, or shut off. Based on my own work with behavior change, I knew we needed to make the concept relevant and actionable, so everyone could recognize and remove the harmful or unnecessary "shoulds" from their lives. I dubbed the pressures as the Should Monster.

It had indeed been a monster in my life, leading me to accept many harmful paradigms that were generating a vortex of self-induced anxiety. What society saw as an adventurous, successful, and happy life was riddled with fatigue and the impossibility of perfectionism under the surface.

I realized my adult existence had largely been an unending attempt to accommodate, hold together, and please others who held different beliefs. Naming the Should Monster and giving it a face allowed me to more easily filter out which advice was helpful and which would be better ignored. For many years, before I began actively battling the Should Monster, I kept up that outward selfie smile because overall, despite the self-induced prison sentence of being a perpetual people-pleaser, I still felt tremendously blessed. My parents taught me to be grateful, no matter what, because things could always be worse. When I slipped up by complaining, it was always immediately followed with guilt for the selfishness of wanting more. I never allowed myself the time to feel emotional pain or expose vulnerability for fear that something would fall through the cracks. It was more important at the time, it seemed, to hold it all together to protect those closest to me. Just keep paying the bills, encouraging the boys, and smiling like a well-mannered Southern woman *should*.

While the major conflicts between being raised with conservative Christian expectations and having the innate desire to conquer the corporate world may seem foreign to those raised in more metropolitan areas, they were, and still are, very real. My liberal grad school roommate, Missy, who was raised in Manhattan, used to poke fun at the stark contrast between the expectations of working women in our two worlds. She especially loved the phrase, "Bless your heart!"—which, as any good Southerner knows, gives one free rein to say ugly things about another person while still appearing ladylike. For example, "She thought her legs would look good in those shorts—bless her heart." Or, "She brought those cookies again that nobody likes—bless her heart."

Over time, I learned that every region and nationality has its own paradigms tied to social ritual or religion. They can be helpful, by establishing safety and order, or harmful, by creating isolation, oppression, and guilt. It's important we learn to identify the difference and choose actions based on our own needs, wants, and values.

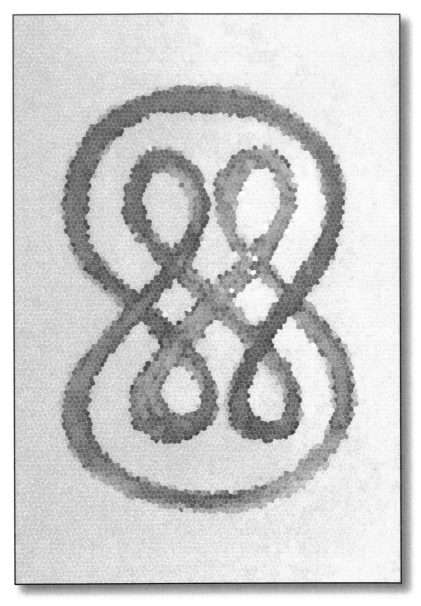

Ancient Infinity Knot

CHAPTER 4

Interrelated

Quantum Cognition: An emerging field that applies quantum theory to model cognitive processes such as information-processing, decision-making, reasoning, judgment, and perception. It is based on the paradigms that contextual dependence of information and reasoning can be mathematically described in the framework of quantum information and probability theories.

I built quite an invisible fortress to protect myself from all those "shoulds" over the years. It was more efficient to be logic-based, believing we choose a meaning to assign to every event, that there is a scientific explanation for everything, and that, ultimately, most things relate to mathematics. As long as there was a logical, science-based explanation for something, I could open my mind to it. After all, music, the Golden Ratio, symmetry, sounds, and even humans are made of nothing more than energy vibrating at varying frequencies. Quantum science has proven that waves only become particles once they're observed—we are, therefore, materializing our own reality at every moment.

Quite the opposite, my best friend, Kay, is almost 100-percent intuition-led and heart-based, believing everything we see at work, home, and in nature is a sign. She is an empath, often unknowingly taking on others' emotions and burdens. This made others feel good around her, but sometimes manifested in issues within her own body if she wasn't careful to protect herself. I met Kay in 2012 when training for my first marathon, the Boston Marathon. She and a host of other wonderful locals from the Hendersonville Running Club (HRC) were seasoned long-distance runners. They shared tips on everything—what could help me improve my times, what to eat before and after the race, where to stop and "go" if duty calls while training, when to arrive at a race, and, most importantly, how to survive the hundreds of miles and hours of training to prepare. They were wonderful!

A nonprofit group, Wake Up Narcolepsy, used the marathon to raise awareness each year for the incurable sleep disorder, narcolepsy. They asked if I'd participate by raising funds and awareness, since our son, Trent, had been recently diagnosed with the disorder. It was a great cause for something I was passionate about supporting, so I gratefully accepted the challenge.

Unfortunately, I had no idea when agreeing to complete the race that the Boston Marathon was for elite athletes who qualified to participate by achieving very fast times in prior races. It was like the Super Bowl of road races, and even though there were thousands of fundraising slots granted each year as an important social benefit from the race, the Should Monster filled me with strong guilt at the thought that, as a first-time marathoner, I would be participating alongside—or should I say *behind*—those who had worked incredibly hard to achieve their acceptance. With great humility and respect to the runners who prequalified, I decided to follow through and meet my commitment to the volunteer group by increasing awareness for narcolepsy, raising funds for research, and doing my best to finish the race.

At 89 degrees, the race was among the hottest on record. To put that in perspective, according to the Northeast Region Climate Center, nearly 70% of Boston Marathon races have occurred at 55 degrees or colder, with 95% of them being 70 degrees and under. There were stations set up every few miles for water and Gatorade, but by the time the "non-runner" runners reached them, most only had warm Gatorade left to offer participants. Over 4,000 runners chose not to race that day, deferring their qualifying slot until the following year. Thousands more that did run were lying on the sides of the road, many in a fetal position from dehydration.

My heart sank as I also witnessed participants being whisked to nearby ERs for heat-related treatment. It wasn't a typical race, but I didn't have any previous experience, so I naively assumed all marathons must have been like that. Even without having water to drink along the way, I needed to ditch my dripping wet knee brace at mile 10, leave my sopping wet socks on the side of the road at mile 17, and stop at a 7-Eleven store around mile 22 for a Dr. Pepper.

Climbing between the rows of cheering onlookers, I weaved my way towards the store with a fellow narcolepsy supporter who had been waiting in the crowd. Someone with better sense would have bought water, but my stomach felt queasy and my grandma had always given me a Dr. Pepper when I felt sick. So, I gulped down the dark soda with at least half of it missing my parched mouth and mingling with the sweat on my already soaked white Wake Up Narcolepsy t-shirt. By the stares from the crowd along the course, you'd have thought this was an uncommon occurrence, but I reasoned if people were allowed to stop mid-race to use the potty, then I should be allowed to stop for a soda to keep from puking in the street. Depositing the empty bottle in a recycling bin, I continued towards the finish line.

With the finish in sight, the crowd began wildly cheering. As I approached, they were inspired, they rose to their feet with elation, they were shouting encouraging remarks as applause erupted. *Was it my soda-stained t-shirt drawing all this attention?* As my astonished grin stretched from ear-to-ear, the man from behind me emerged to my side. Dripping wet with exhaustion, he was steps away from completing the entire 26.2 miles during one of the hottest Boston Marathon race days on record while pushing his paralyzed son. The young teen smiled with glee from underneath his race day hat as an American flag flapped brilliantly behind his wheelchair.

This man had demonstrated a most unselfish love for his son. He had run in nearly unbearable conditions without adequate supplies of water and was just about to cross the finish line. I was humbled, inspired, and filled with joy for the opportunity to have witnessed such a beautiful and powerful experience for both father and son! I slowed my own pace and joined the swell of overwhelming cheers in support. I trotted across the finish line, where each participant ducked into a finisher's medal being donned by volunteers, promptly exited my sneakers, tied their laces together and hung them around my neck where they dangled against the medal on the walk back to the hotel. I was in a bit of shock from dehydration and fatigue.

A friend from the nonprofit group stopped by to check on me and see if I was all right. By this time, I was shaking from a serious loss of water and calories and pain and nausea had taken over. I asked him to do what any logical person would do in that situation: "I really need you to go to any lengths necessary to find some mashed potatoes and another Dr. Pepper." It seemed like the only things that could help me recover. After a shower and some food, I felt normal again and could check the box—marathon one was complete. I vowed it would be a long time before I did something like *that* again but quickly changed my mind. There's something addictive about setting each goal, training for it, and then completing the race. And, while I did complete the race, to this day I still choose to honor Boston Marathon qualifiers by not wearing the prestigious jersey given to participants.

After that race, I grew close to several of the local runners and continued to complete many other races. Kay and I usually spent our Saturday mornings and Wednesday nights running or practicing hot yoga. Both in our 40s, we have nearly identical physique types, but she felt energized by soaking up the sun with her beautiful brown skin. Meanwhile, I never left the house without sunscreen, even on a cloudy day. This echoed the way we each interacted with spirituality.

Kay felt and processed everything. It all had meaning, and she consulted her heart to uncover it. In contrast, I insisted her focus was what actually attracted events to occur, because she was getting on the same wavelength with what she expected. In other words, what she saw as a sign from the universe, I saw as manifestation of focused thought. Depending on the meaning we assign to occurrences, sometimes a synchronistic event had positive results, and at other times, negative results. We had many lively debates and grew in mutual understanding of our different approaches about whether things have a meaning intrinsically or whether we assign the meanings as we go. Our friendship grew stronger and our perspectives began to reshape. Over many years of research and discovery about the behavior of energy, quantum science, and the power of belief, I learned that we were both right.

One of the most memorable races Kay and I ran together was the Rocket City Marathon, in Huntsville, Alabama, on a cold December day in 2013. We carb-loaded with Mellow Mushroom pizza the night before the event. Carb-loading involves using athletic events as an excuse to eat anything you want the day before to fuel up. We were too short on time to grab breakfast on the morning of race day but luckily, she had saved the remaining pizza from the night before (I tossed everything; she kept it—another one of our differences). I couldn't get past the texture of the cold, slimy pizza that had been in the car overnight but managed to choke down some crust. I took the edges; she ate the center before the 26.2 miles ahead of us. Like our appreciation for consulting intuition itself, she was feasting on its flavor while at the time I was comfortable just nibbling at its edges.

We made it to the starting gate just minutes before the race. The IT (Iliotibial) band in my left knee was injured from overuse. The knee was obviously swollen, but given my stubborn resolve, it wouldn't be me if I didn't run anyhow. Kay gently placed her left palm on my swollen knee and her right hand low towards the ground. Fellow racers in the starting gate wondered what in the world we were up to. Like siphoning gas from a car tank, she pumped the inflamed heat energy from my knee and out into the universe as I felt an oozy sensation of warmth flowing out of my body and into her hand. Surely this was some sort of magic trick! I stood there, ever the logical skeptic, pain free and in utter disbelief at my now normally sized knee.

I thought about this miracle throughout the race. There had to be an explanation. I'd never seen or experienced anything like it. What did the onlookers think? What would people say if I shared this phenomenon with them? They'd think I was even more nuts than they already did. But, what if this could help my son's illness? Kay told me the technique was one of many alternative healing practices she learned after the death of her fiancé. She was referred to the practice to help cope with the grief and, as a science teacher, she began studying it through the Healing Beyond Borders collection of educational programs in earnest. This was the first time I had heard about her capability with energy healing. The National Institutes of Health classified the work as biofield therapy. Fascinated and full of enthusiasm to use some form of this therapy to help my son, I began taking courses as well.

I was a professional Certified Energy Manager who studied electrical engineering as part of the credentialing process, so after learning that biofield therapy leverages the body's natural electrical and magnetic attributes, the healing technique used on my knee made total sense to me—the negative charge in her left palm attracted the thermal energy and the positive charge in her right hand, coupled with gravity, naturally drew then drained the heat. It was similar to an application of the Second Law of Thermodynamics. Simple physics, and I completely understood this "magic"!

An insatiable curiosity to know more about these and similar techniques drove me to consume books, courses, and formal training. I first studied vibrational medicine, consuming many books and research papers on the groundbreaking scientific work. Then I completed four levels of the same Bioenergy Field certifications that Kay had. The studies combined energy-healing techniques from ancient Eastern cultures, Hopi Native Americans, Japanese Reiki traditions, and even the findings of a modern-day NASA physicist.

Ultimately, I finished the program's Bioenergy Field 100-hour practicum (as classified by the North American Nursing Diagnosis Association). After dozens of hours of practice, I began to tap into a form of natural intuition and could often see and feel energy fields around people, trees, animals, and anything living. As a certified scuba diver, I even noticed energy around sea life, even though the light and electrical characteristics under the water reacted differently than in the air. My belief in the spiritual, unseen powers within and around us grew stronger because they began to make sense in a new, logic-driven light that proved physical and quantum science reinforced spiritual beliefs, like prayer and healing. It also explained why in ancient and modern-day religious ceremonies, they laid hands on someone in need of healing or blessing.

I began to observe and study the interrelatedness of everything from social and psychological models to colors, musical notes, relationships, and the body's natural vortexes of energy, called chakras. Further, that everything within and around us simply boils down to various energetic frequencies. To simplify the concepts, lower frequencies represent more basic physical and psychological needs, while higher frequencies are used for more complex physical or psychological achievements. Using these scientific principles, it made sense that some on the autism spectrum could actually "hear" music coming from something they were seeing, like a landscape. Their wiring simply gave them different frequencies to which they may tune in.

The more I learned about quantum science, vibrational medicine, and ancient energetic healing techniques, the more it reinforced the common threads among many spiritual beliefs. This omnipresent, all-knowing Spirit had been recognized and written about for millennia and inspired many peaceful world religions. It made sense why there were so many striking similarities between spiritual beliefs around the world. One likeness is this notion of an endless energy source that lives both outside of and within each of us. Another is that the resource is innate and always present to tap into for wisdom, love, intuition, guidance, and peace. This unconditional energy source can be used to ignite personal power within and to strengthen our communities. Our shared source of energy is an opportunity to come together globally, rather than quibble over our differences.

Quantum principles, genetically mapped electrical vibrations, and shared sinusoidal waves (continuous mathematical cadence) explained the natural rhythm in all living things and our ability to connect to the non-physical through spirituality—it all came back to energy. As I attended the funeral of a family friend, I thought of Albert Einstein's famous quote, "Energy cannot be created or destroyed; it can only be changed from one form to another." That assertion also supports faith-based beliefs that our spirit lives on after death. It transitions to somewhere or something else. What some may have dismissed as religious storytelling can now clearly be explained with modern science. We each choose individual beliefs based upon our upbringing, experiences, or education, but are all born as "energists."

The same energy that joins communities, creates light, produces healing, inspires prayer, and fuels our transportation also powers our minds and bodies. Just think of all the ways our language describes feelings that relate directly to our condition of being electric! We describe ourselves as: bright, burnt out, spun up, on fire, lighting up a room, creating a vibe, glowing, in sync, transformed, and countless other related words.

Believing in the spirit is easier when it's understood that *everything* about us and around us is energy-based. Since the future is simply a series of waves that become reality as we observe them, we have the ability to design our own filters, beliefs, and reactions—regardless of the onslaught of distractions. The energy inside us has been described as many things in various cultures such as Chi (Chinese), Prana (Hindus), or the Holy Spirit (Christians).

For Christians, the King James Bible is the most popular English interpretation of original Greek and Hebrew scriptures. This collection of scriptures references God and Christ as the "Light" 272 times and makes clear that humans were shaped in God's image. Modern quantum science reinforces these ancient beliefs by proving energy is the source of all living things. It is available 24 hours a day and 7 days a week, plus it has no costs, can heal through natural physics, and it serves as the ultimate renewable resource to recharge mentally, physically, and spiritually.

I realized, during this time of learning, that I'd experienced glimpses of this inner and outer spirit world long before—like as a kid how I played the piano by allowing the vibrational sequences in my head and heart to come through my hands and onto the keys. If I stopped to think about what I was playing, I goofed. It was not a logically explainable ability, but rather a gift that flowed forth without conscious thought. Understanding the sources, characteristics, and science of electricity affirmed inextricable, inspiring, and exciting connections beyond wires and solar panels; it exposed the life-affirming truth that energy is the source of *everything*. All I knew at that point was that I wanted to tap into it more deeply, understand its power, and identify a way to share it with others.

Breathe Deeply

CHAPTER 5

It's Getting Hot in Here

Energy, etymology: The word "energy" comes from the Greek "en" (in, within) plus "ergon" (work), so in its simplest form, energy is defined as the power inherent within to do work.

We all are driven by a passion of some sort: teachers to educate, firefighters to rescue, business leaders to increase shareholder value, performers to entertain, and so on. My passion shifted in the early 2000s from developing leading-edge financial systems (before PayPal existed) to creating sustainable technology and energy solutions in an effort to help as many animals, plants, and waterways as possible—oh yeah, and humans, too. Getting things done, a willingness to risk looking stupid, inventing the promotions I wanted, and stubborn optimism were key ingredients in the secret sauce to attaining leadership positions near the top of two large global companies. I was following my heart and somehow had managed to get paid for it.

Leveraging innovation to drive sustainability, renewable energy, and engagement was fun, fulfilling, and paid the bills all at once. It felt great. It was fun to ride the wave of new technologies whose adoption ushered in smarter use of resources—whether financial, natural, or human. The more I learned about energy, the more I valued its absolute power. And my conviction for using energy mindfully, responsibly, and respectfully was itself electric.

However, my passion for renewable energy solutions was not shared throughout much of the U.S., so I focused on development of profitable, efficient business models rather than sustainability. In fact, I jokingly called sustainability the "S-word" because it was so polarizing. In 2007, I had the opportunity to represent the built sector as a collaborator on the Presidential Climate Action Plan. The team created tangible priorities that would help improve the quality of life for Americans and other living things domestically. This group had been working on pollution awareness and energy solutions for a couple of decades. They shaped policies, influenced industry practices, and collaborated with top CEOs, forward-thinking innovators, best-selling authors, and Hollywood influencers—they were revered as pioneers, visionaries, and futurists. To my surprise, many of them were also cranky, cynical, and all-around negative. New ideas were often accompanied with eye rolls and seasoned sarcastic statements, like "Yeah, *that* will never be adopted." At the time, I was brimming with newfound purpose and enthusiasm, so it was confusing.

I knew that to stay positive amidst the cynicism would be critical to success. I focused almost entirely on the tangible economic benefits from renewable investments or energy efficiencies, turning real estate assets into more profitable operations with additional opportunities for revenue. Sadly, it was the only way to create meaningful change—focusing on the *money* it would make or save. I felt my financial and technical background had given me a unique perspective to relate to businesspeople in a way that was important to them.

One of my most intrinsically rewarding projects was convincing our company to build a net-zero community on the Tennessee-Kentucky border where the homes would produce as much energy, on average, as they consumed during the year. It was the first of its kind for government housing. But the pinnacle of my energy career came later with a different company as we christened the world's largest solar rooftop-powered community at Fort Bliss in Texas.

For every high, there was an equal low. The press made sure Americans heard about the Exxon Valdez oil spill in Alaska in 1989 and the BP Gulf oil spill of 2010 that spewed 4.9 million barrels of crude oil into the waters off Florida and Alabama, creating an outcry of awareness. Ironically, the press made nary a peep about a spill at the Kingston TVA Plant, around Christmastime of 2008, which was 10 times the size of the BP Gulf spill and 100 times the size of the Exxon Valdez disaster. There were too many investments and subsidies in the coal industry, so the people in power couldn't risk exposing the industry's dangerous risks inside America's heartland.

The Kingston spill covered 300 acres of land, flowed into waterways, destroyed homes, and left land uninhabitable, killing untold numbers of animals and fish. Cleanup-crew members exposed to the spill's toxic coal ash developed fatal diseases, including brain cancer, lung cancer, and leukemia. And 10 years following the spill, more than 40 workers had died from spill-related illnesses. Invisible forces of power and greed worked not only to hide the dirty underbelly of the fossil fuels industry, but also to quash news of positive progress in renewable energy. For instance, the clean energy market in the U.S. grew by roughly five times the rate of the overall economy during those years. But a constant, steady deluge of ads and messaging from clever marketing folks were highly effective in hiding the facts so the disproportionately high subsidies for fossil fuels would continue to flow and high-dollar investors would keep raking in the cash.

The environment is shared by all nations and political parties, yet it was ironic how politicized climate change had become. During speaking engagements, I often pointed out that some of the most powerful, groundbreaking environmental legislation was led by Republicans such as Richard Nixon, George W. Bush, and Sarah Palin. Most people, including Republicans, don't realize this. Vice President Gore created an internationally award-winning documentary about climate change, and because of his political affiliation, the environmental movement began to be associated with Democrats only. It didn't make sense.

Politics and its resulting polarization went a long way to kill meaningful education about our impact on the environment. It's about the *health* of humans and other living things. I just couldn't comprehend why that was so difficult to understand when the evidence—in the forms of the growing number of pollution-related asthma and cancer cases, for example—was so prolific and irrefutable.

Perhaps the most valuable lesson I learned in change management was that fighting against something people don't want to change is like the Third Newtonian Law of Motion: Nobody makes progress because both sides cancel out each other's energy. So, we focused efforts on positive economic solutions that brought benefits to all sides, a win-win approach. The language of the dollar was understood and welcomed by all. It allowed us to get behind a desire already in motion—creating shareholder wealth—and accelerate it forward.

But as time wore on, fewer swaths of the American public wanted to hear about clean energy and sustainability. It became even more politically divisive. After a decade of tiptoeing around skeptics and fighting to maintain hope despite the dire scientific truths, I understood viscerally what those cynical environmental experts must have felt. I became bone-tired from pouring proverbial thimbles of water onto a raging forest fire. Like an eerie dream, it was as if despite the impending heat of an approaching forest fire, many friends and colleagues just bought more marshmallows to roast in its flame.

This constant conflict of being compelled to protect our natural resources and health, while deeply understanding the enormity of the problem of climate change and the financial resources reinforcing it, was quietly taking its toll on me. Frustration turned to sadness when in 2017 our own federal government repealed years of legislation that protected our air and waterways. Is our own health of less value than winning a political pissing match? I no longer could relate.

Our political positions had become a circus, and the precious environment supporting all life was being treated as a side show. We went beyond repealing domestic policies and withdrew support of international treaties that protected the well-being of our societies globally. Spending more than 15 years drawing attention to something that enormous financial contributors wanted hidden was like trying to stand up in emotional quicksand—over time it swallowed up my enthusiasm and slowly began to bury my hope.

Hazard Ahead

CHAPTER 6

!Warning! Shock Hazard

Second Law of Thermodynamics: As pressure is applied to a system, it becomes more disorderly and releases heat energy, so it becomes colder. A disordered system cannot get back into its original state, but the molecules released during change may form into something more orderly with newly found energy.

While I struggled with burnout at work and wondered if the career I had chosen was simply a wasted effort, my concerns about my sons' health continued to escalate. Not having control of their suffering, and worse, not being able to fix their health problems, despite hard work and stubborn optimism, would have been crushing … to someone who allowed themselves to *feel* their emotions. While there were some moments when I scheduled a few minutes of grief, mostly, it was like a surreal TV drama series where unbelievable, impossible situations were hurled at the heroine, but she used her trusty invisible shield to ward them off. Allowing myself to *feel* the events surely would have acknowledged they were not only real, but had also managed to conquer us. Yet in my heroine's show, the theme song "We will not surrender!" echoed deep in my subconscious.

In my paradigm, feeling pain and showing emotions equated to being weak. As a young child, I was taught that the primary goal was not to screw up in the first place. If I did, and began to look as if I might shed a tear, Dad would warn, "If you don't wipe that sad look off your face, I'll *give* you something to cry about." As a businesswoman, I focused on portraying confidence, logic, and control. So I told myself, *Look, I realize your sons are sick, but you've made it this far. Don't blow it by getting all emotional now, for goodness' sake. Don't get weak. People look to you for strength and inspiration, so show up and do so powerfully.*

As if Ethan's rare knee condition wasn't enough, years after his surgeries, he began having severe, debilitating migraines. Upon months of investigating, we finally learned he had a cognitive vision impairment that prevented him from being able to read or perceive depth normally. At the time, he was on the backside of high school, so the kid had somehow managed to make it through all of those years of learning without being able to normally decipher the information projected at the front of the room or written in the textbooks. Quite literally, his visual perception was unique, so he processed information from a completely different perspective. Over time, Ethan's knees grew strong enough to walk, but we knew it was unlikely he would ever fully run again.

Trent's narcolepsy took visiting eight doctors and a trip across the country to the top sleep center at Stanford University to finally receive a proper diagnosis and treatment. Years earlier, as a 14-year-old, he had begun flight training and logging hours, certain he would someday fly professionally. Narcolepsy stole his dreams of becoming a pilot and entering military service, forever changing the path of his life. Trent finished the last half of high school teaching himself at home and grasping to find hope again within this new future.

It was one unfortunate, uncontrollable, unfixable event after another. There was nothing else I could do to help my sons, and the weight of that felt like the worst kind of failure.

A long-expected and amicable divorce ended over two decades of marriage the same year that empty nesting began. Charlie returned to his hometown to continue his passion of running a boutique family farm and business. The farm brings great joy to kids of all ages and my parents still volunteer there on occasion during peak season. Trent finished getting his pilot's license, and although he could not fly commercially, he used his passion for flight to man commercial drones for a civil engineering company in St. Louis. And Ethan was accepted to an elite art college in Detroit where he began working as an artist at the Ford Museum, refining his glass-blowing skills.

It was deafeningly quiet.

Around Christmas that year, I was surprised during a routine doctor visit to discover I had skin cancer. This tiny spot on the surface of my back required digging a hole so deep that it reached between my ribs. This relatively quick fix that required three layers of stitches became a trigger on every medical chart, so routine tests of other types began checking more carefully for the "C" word.

Suspicious tissue found in a mammogram a few months later left me with the options to wait and see if it manifested into cancer, risking a full mastectomy, or remove the tissue immediately. I was stunned, but grateful my doctor caught the potential for something more serious early. I told the surgeon to take what she needed to get the potentially precancerous tissue removed. Within a few weeks, it had been methodically and clinically handled. It all happened so fast.

In what I thought was the brave and unselfish style of a heroine, I kept the entire process on a need-to-know basis. It was a lot of change all at once, even for a change agent like me. The surgery was not at all what I expected—it was worse. There were little drainage hoses running out of my body into pumps on each side. There were stitches in every direction. I learned to sleep like Dracula, flat on my back with hands folded neatly across my ribcage, to prevent getting tangled in the tubes and tape.

Righty turned out smaller than lefty, as there was more tissue that had to be removed on that side. Follow-up screenings, in which my body was contorted onto machines in painful and unnatural ways, were required to be sure no suspicious tissue remained. To say I was being tested mentally, emotionally, and physically would be an understatement. But despite fleeting moments of fear, sadness, frustration, loneliness—I stuck to my longtime habits: Bury emotions, show strength, and don't cry. Refusing to give up perceived control—and to subconsciously prove I was still whole—I ran a half marathon less than three weeks after the major surgery.

I can't say I'm thrilled with losing half of my boobs, but we should give ourselves a break about our bodies. None of us are perfect. As my friend, comedian Jennifer Anglin, would say, "We are all flawed *and* awesome—we're flawesome!"

As I struggled with ways to think positively of my flawesome new silhouette in the mirror, I realized many of the "shoulds" that had long hemmed me in had transitioned out of my life. In the aftermath of divorce, empty nesting, and a cancer scare, I no longer had to fit into a cookie-cutter version of being the perfect mom or wife. I felt a weight lifted, a sliver of light peeking in, as though a door cracked open and something blindingly bright was on the other side.

I snapped the door closed on the daydream and returned my attention to my reflection, my new body. I thought about something my mother used to say about beauty: "There is nothing—I mean *nothing*—more attractive than a genuine smile." It's true. We can be at our worst and a heartfelt smile still warms those around us. Science even proves that our brains think differently when smile muscles are activated, so the benefits help ourselves as much as others. I resolved that henceforth my beauty would come from within.

I did not tell anyone at work what happened with my breast surgery. I did share with my boss that I needed a procedure to remove some potentially cancer-causing cells. He was unbelievably flexible and supportive. Not long after surgery, nobody could tell there were tubes and bandages underneath my suit jacket as I sat alongside 20 other global executives during a negotiations training session. The mandatory course was a series of competitive individual and team bargaining scenarios recommended for leaders from our company and others.

I was atop the leaderboard thus far, which simultaneously helped me gain recognition from the course director and put me in the crosshairs of a disrespectful male in the class who would rather roll in poison ivy than admit to being outwitted by a female. We were challenged to deploy negotiating tactics after the first day of learning. The next morning, another participant shared with the class how I had successfully bargained for our dinner group to receive free appetizers and desserts the previous evening.

When the instructor asked me to share my techniques for success with the other executives, the disrespectful classmate, a card-carrying member of the stale pale male club that no longer led, but still influenced our sector, interjected, "She probably just took off her shirt and used her tits!" A few uncomfortable chuckles leaked out in the room. But *nobody.* Said. A Single. Word. Including me. Imagine how it felt to experience the snipe while still healing from losing half of them. Perhaps another time I would've had a witty retort, but I was just too tired. Something subtle inside reached its tipping point in that moment and gently snapped.

Riding High

CHAPTER 7

Shed Your Skin

Snake: For millennia, snakes have symbolized healing powers.
A universal sign for medicine and healing, the Caduceus, comes
from the Greek god Aesclepius. According to tradition, the snake
totem enters your life to awaken your healing abilities and encourage
spiritual liberation while promoting growth and transition.

I was very close to my mom's mother, Alma. At 4'11" and around 200 pounds, she looked like an adorable cherubic doll. We once rode an elephant together at Circus World—she showed no fear. Driving a lime-green Vega we called The Green Fly, she typically went *way* over the speed limit, much to my delight. I spent a lot of time in the summers with Grandma learning to stitch, paint, make quilts, and all sorts of creative things. I made friends with the giant sheepdog, Ralph, across the road, and enjoyed doing flips from end to end of her enormous front lawn to entertain rural passersby.

Grandma was an incredible cook—beans and cornbread, roast beef, and chocolate fudge were regulars. She always let us have our own little garden spots during the summer that we would plant and tend together. Grandma had a plethora of perennials, my favorite of which were the deep purple irises nested in the fencerow. They had periwinkle blue stamens and a velvety texture you couldn't resist touching. It was the kind of place where dreams were free to grow. I sat on the back porch and envisioned getting married to a marvelous man someday in the woods just beyond the backyard. We'd be on horseback for the ceremony and I'd wear a dark purple dress and sneakers. (Who needs tradition?!) He would be kind and handsome. And he would be my best friend who would experience many new adventures with me.

Alma passed away the summer before my junior year of high school. I'm not sure if it was because of being raised in the Christian faith or because of my own intuition, but I did not acknowledge her death as an ending, but rather a transition from our physical visits to an ongoing spiritual connectedness. Over the remaining years at home, and throughout adulthood, she remained a steady source of peace and direction. I never forgot the joy I felt around her and how it gave me freedom to fantasize about the life I wanted to create. So when I felt particularly frustrated, I still talked to her, even though she had transitioned into a spiritual realm. The calm, guiding presence she had always provided was still there, just in a different form that usually leveraged some sort of animal as her interpreter.

During the final years of my marriage, before Ethan left for college, things became very strained. The friendship Charlie and I enjoyed during our early years had morphed into constant frustration. My birthday, Valentine's Day, and anniversaries were avoided while he watched reruns of his favorite childhood TV series that brought back memories from a brighter time. He refused going to counselors over the years and tossed aside books suggested by them or by me as rubbish or selfish. The pain and resentment in his heart, triggered by the death of his beloved father, had grown like a giant snowball for over a decade. Despite all the work I had done successfully with behavior change in communities, I failed miserably at it in our own home. I focused on the things I could control—my work, my studies of energy, my faith in the Spirit, and our sons' well-being.

While most of the people who studied electrical energy were engineers or investors, and seemed to be relatively similar, the people who studied human bioenergy ranged dramatically. There were physics experts, nurses, massage therapists, business executives, grandmothers, and others. Some of them actively saw their spirit guides, including animals. When first exposed to this motley family of practitioners, I strongly wanted to see something, too—to see Grandma again and to find my own spirit animal. There was so much curiosity about this unknown world, so I eagerly asked them how to see or get to know a personal spirit guide.

While there was no infallible methodology that worked for everyone, the common theme was to "ask the Spirit" during meditation or just prior to bed at night and then listen with an open mind and heart. So, night after night, I prayed at bedtime, often adding a P.S. to Grandma, *I don't want to bother God with this, but will you show me my spirit animal? I can't seem to tune into it. I just know it will be a powerful tiger or a fierce lion, but I could use a little more comfort in my life and really want to connect.*

For several weeks, nothing happened. Tensions at home were higher than ever, and I kept asking for that powerful spirit puma to be revealed. In the middle of the night, a noisy owl outside my window appeared. I'd never seen an owl outside of a zoo before and definitely not at our home in the middle of a subdivision in the suburbs. This one was a Great Horned Owl, just short of two feet in height but large on volume with his one-sided conversations. The sound was more of a loud "hoo-hoo-hoo... hoo" than the classic "hoot" sound one may expect, sort of like a deeply reverberating pigeon sound.

I vividly remember being irritated with him for waking me, finding it hard to go back to sleep. I fussed at him through the window for disturbing my dreams. *Didn't he realize I needed these dreams? I may miss the big revelation of my spirit puma or tiger or lion.* Big cats had always been my favorite animal, so that's why I assumed a spirit animal of mine would likely be some variety of giant, powerful feline.

But he didn't go away. In fact, in addition to midnight visits, the owl also began appearing when Charlie would verbally escalate his frustrations at me. The owl would alight right outside the bedroom window and hoot loudly until the yelling stopped. At one point, Charlie halted in the heat of the moment and in equal parts anger and laughter at the absurdity of the owl's incessant interruptions said, "OK, there's just something too weird about that stupid owl of yours. I don't know what you're feeding him to get him to come out there and hoot at me, but I'm getting sick of it."

Charlie was an animal lover too. It was one of the things that drew me to him more than 20 years ago. He was a good person at heart; he just hadn't taken the time to sort out how to rediscover his own peace and happiness. It wasn't until he made that connection for me that the switch was flipped. I realized that the protective, majestic owl *was* my spirit animal. He had been showing up for weeks, right outside my window, and yet I hadn't been listening with an open mind and heart.

From that point on, I knew deep in my bones that the owl was my spirit animal, and that I needed to practice listening. My physical world was about achieving, making things happen, and getting answers fast. It was about being able to Google something or take a course and obtain the knowledge required at any instant. In contrast, when dialoguing with spiritual energy, it was less about the zeal of seeking and more about becoming a passive receiver by tuning into the unique frequency of the answer. Wired to be action-oriented and ever logical, this was very difficult for me and would take years of practice. When my husband moved out of the house, I never saw that owl again, but I have carried my Inner Owl within ever since.

While everyone will relate to a different person, spirit, or animal in his or her unique way, this owl became my personal symbol of wisdom, the representation for tapping into the abundant source of universal energy for peace, joy, protection, unconditional love, and guidance. It wasn't until researching the Great Horned Owl six years after my encounter with him outside my window that I discovered early naturalists dubbed it the "winged tiger" or "tiger owl" because of its striped pattern, ferocity, and hunting skills. It seemed I had received a version of my beloved big cat, after all.

After my marriage to Charlie ended, I asked Grandma, "Will I ever feel love like people do in the movies, or is it impossible to get through this hard shell surrounding my heart?" She sent cardinals. They began hanging out on my back porch, in trees along the cycling route, and would appear—up to four red males at a time—during races. My friends, except for Kay, couldn't believe it, because the sheer numbers of them were an impossibility. We had no idea what the bright red birds meant at the time. All we knew was, for some reason, the answer to my question would involve cardinals.

In the aftermath of the cancer scare, I put more questions out into the universe, sometimes in the form of prayers and at other times it was more of a mental conversation requesting input from Grandma. A couple things weighing on my mind were my career and my name. The career had been a great adventure and quite successful, but it felt like being an advocate for a healthy environment had been dismissed as political silliness. *Should I try something else—and if so, what?* My married name had literally become a brand for which a simple Google search validated my accomplishments, certifications, published works, and career highlights. Changing back to my original birth name would mean entirely reinventing my credibility. Unsure how she would answer me, I soon realized the responses would continue to come through a variety of animals, beginning with a rattlesnake I didn't see.

Don was a seasoned design and construction colleague who became my friend. He was also an experienced hiker. Don is the one who introduced me to the activity in earnest. We spent many days climbing, snacking, and appreciating nature, up to 18 miles of mountain trails at a time. We rarely talked much as we each used the peace of the woods and all its animals—even a cougar on one occasion—to calm our constantly racing and revolving minds. Formerly a surveyor, Don had a visual scanning method that allowed him to see obstacles, like spider webs and critters. Since he kept a constant eye on our direction, it made sense that he nearly always led and I followed. While used to leading in the office, I was happier hiking in the back—missing the spider webs in remote areas, avoiding the duty of staying on the right trail, and getting to completely shift into mental neutral.

For these reasons, it was rare that I would have been walking in front, but about halfway through an advanced 10-mile hike at Savage Gulf in

Tennessee's South Cumberland State Park, I decided to trot ahead and was hoofing it up an incline when, abruptly, Don snatched me by the pack strapped around my shoulders and jerked me backwards into the air. As my adrenaline kicked in, I watched a rattlesnake fly between my legs from the hillside to our right. The agitated snake stayed on the trail and eventually had to be coaxed along with a long stick. We took photos because my son Ethan raised snakes and would know what type she was and why she was being so aggressive. He confirmed it was a rattler and said she was likely gravid, so the snake was just in protective mother mode.

It wasn't until months later I learned that given our distance from the truck (about 5 miles of challenging hiking) and the lack of accessibility to medical care, I owe Don at least my right leg and possibly my life—who knew?! I was under the impression that if I'd been bitten, we could just suck out the venom like John Wayne did in the old Western movies.

Over a series of hikes, when exhausted and deep in the woods, I would ask the Spirit and Grandma for guidance. Raised Methodist and Baptist, having conversations with the Spirit was normal. I figured since Alma was in that space of universal energy, I may as well ask the whole committee. The question remained: *What should I do about my career?* After all, my work was always the controllable aspect of my life. It grounded me, challenged me, and gave me a continued sense of purpose, especially since the boys were grown and gone.

But what was once a passionate purpose had grown more and more painful. It became tough to keep climbing the steep hill of environmental awareness while being tugged down constantly by the gravity of the fact that many top U.S. leaders and corporate decision-makers believed sustainability to be unimportant. Short-term and short-sighted signals to the stock market outweighed long-term economic and environmental health. Asthma and death rates accelerated at the most alarming rate in history. Type 2 diabetes became linked to fossil-fuel pollution.

Tens of thousands of species became unnaturally extinct as if someone flicked the delicately spinning top representing their naturally interconnected life cycles. And it wasn't only that we used too much pesticide to *treat* our basic foods, it was that our genetically modified (GMO) grains actually had *become* a pesticide. It kept me up at night. It broke my heart. Add on the decades of disrespectful corporate cultures, the lack of down time, and the self-imposed "shoulds" of perfectionism—I realized, for the first time in my life, that work was no longer my solace.

In successive months, more snakes followed. I saw them when walking through the neighborhood, riding bicycles with friends, and hiking. Up until this time in my life, I had maybe experienced three snakes in the wild. It was obviously not normal to come across so many. One day hiking with Don at Big South Fork in southern Kentucky, we saw *five* snakes. They were different shapes and sizes. Some of them politely posed for Facebook photos, but others were camera shy. The signs were clear, but I could not decode the message. It started to become a joke amongst my closest friends.

Especially odd was the fact that on the day we saw five snakes, Don didn't see most of the little crawlers until I pointed them out. One went directly between his legs as he walked. They were clearly there for me. I would literally be asking Grandma for a sign and another snake would appear around the corner. I asked spiritually connected friends, read books, Googled for answers, but none of the answers made sense. *What in the world was she trying to tell me?* It no longer mattered if people thought I was crazy, if they didn't understand this mystical interaction, because these messages were intended for me and I was utterly curious to decode them.

One day while cycling on the rural roads near home, I was at the end of my rope. I needed to make some decisions about my job and didn't know what to do. On one hand, I had become exhausted trying to make a difference, yet it did not seem to be valued. On the other hand, I had a wonderful boss and a great paycheck.

"What should I do?" I spoke aloud in desperation to the universe, and a snake so long that he stretched across the entire road crossed lazily in front of my bike. I unclipped my cleat from the pedal and stood dumbfounded as he passed, clearly nonchalant for interrupting my ride.

Tears of frustration welling in my eyes, I remounted the bike and started pedaling fast. Angry and confused, I was trying to outrun the frustration and comprehend this weird message … powering up the hills … faster and faster, heart racing … it hit me.

"*Shed your skin.*"

So simple. So right there in front of my face this entire time! Shed your skin. Snakes shed their skin for two reasons: first, to allow for growth. Unlike other creatures, a snake's skin doesn't stretch, so to grow, it has to let go of the old parts that were restricting its maturity. It made perfect sense that the career that once invigorated me was now holding me back, and that the perceptions from others I allowed to guide my own decision-making had drowned out my own intuition. And my name … I was worried about having to reinvent myself, but realized there are no limits to the number of times we may do precisely that. I was being given the opportunity for rebirth, for growth, for expanding into anything I wanted to be.

The second reason a snake sheds its skin is to rid itself of parasites. How many parasites had I acquired over the years? Perhaps it was the guy who removed my name from a corporate sustainability report that I had spent months creating for our home office overseas and replaced it with his own, only to be dumb enough to leave it on the shared office printer. How long had that been going on? Or maybe it was the unhealthy relationships I accommodated to be nice or the beautiful home that surrounded me with so many painful memories. *Holy shit! Shed your skin, and get rid of it all. I get it. Message received, and thank you.* I felt a great deal of gratitude for this guidance.

Over the years of self-imposed pressure and busyness, this feeling of connectedness with God, with fellow Americans, and with myself declined to the point that faking it was no longer an option. Like Pink Floyd's song, my old self had become comfortably numb. What was I running from? Or to? It's not something I'd ever stood still enough to listen for or to allow through the impenetrable force field long enough to deliberate. Each day the door to my heart was closing further until, at some point, feeling at all had become so elusive that I wondered if my capacity to feel pain, hope, sadness, joy, and, most importantly, love, still existed at all.

How would I describe this state of being numb? It was like being on cruise control when driving on a long road trip. You got the car to that speed where you were exceeding the boundaries of the speed limit but not so much that you drew the attention of law enforcement. Next, you shifted your mind to other things like a new audiobook, a podcast, your favorite playlist, or a conversation with the passenger next to you to distract yourself from the passing miles.

Being emotionally numb was like driving through life at a high speed and being vaguely aware of the things whizzing by, but not actively experiencing the speed bumps, the curves, or the subtle accelerations and decelerations. The focus was squarely on the next destination, not the journey, which was left to autopilot. Stopping along the way was limited to biological needs, not for the joy of it, and upon arriving at the journey's end, you realized many waypoints along the path were passed by without even noticing.

Pregnant with emptiness, and much to the shock and horror of my friends and family, I quit my well-paying job without a backup plan, changed my name, put my house on the market, and began giving away the things inside it. While I respected their opinions, it felt liberating, rather than devastating, to remove the things that were no longer moving my life forward. It was time to begin enjoying the trip itself in addition to the destination.

Blindingly Bright Dreams

CHAPTER 8

Tuning Out

Finding Frequencies: An AM radio only needs 1.7 megahertz of frequency; while, deep-space radio communications require a minimum of 2,290 megahertz. You can tune in to and out of different messages, based on the complexity, importance, and magnitude of the messages for which you seek.

Like a radio, our days are filled with thousands of channels, each with its own frequency. A barrage of information broadcasts through ads, calls, emails, and the opinions of those around us. In fact, I believe data is now the single most powerful commodity—ahead of gold, fiat currency, and even electricity—because it enables greater personalization and relevance than ever possible in the past. We are told how to think, who to love, and what we should look like. It is overwhelming.

We choose what to tune in to based on our own experiences. Perhaps we listen to what's most entertaining, or the message parroted the loudest, or the people with whom we are most in sync mentally, physically or spiritually. Until we are mindful of how we're choosing to allow information inside our minds, we're blindly accepting the influx through our own biased filters. This is particularly important for leaders to recognize so they don't subconsciously tune out or exclude the contributions from others who think or look differently. It speaks to the power of leveraging diversity and inclusion in work, community, and home settings.

A famous psychological study by Solomon Asch showed that a third of the time, people knowingly gave the wrong answer in order to fit in with others—proving the profound impact of our desire to please others and feel a sense of belonging. Being mindful means choosing which opinions, ads, emails, and influences we allow to affect us—and staying true to what you know is right, even if it means standing alone. This process of mindfully choosing what messages to tune in to would help me identify what was causing stress, disconnection, frustration, and anxiety. Using this filter would also help me tune out the Should Monster.

I decided to switch off my daily routines and head far away. Somehow, I thought distance would help me tap into that deep, unending source of intuition and finally gain clarity on the next steps leading to fulfillment. Even if clarity never came, at least I would know that my next decisions would be influenced only by my God and myself.

With my love of nature and adventure, disappearing into the wilderness seemed like a great idea. Unfortunately, now unemployed, finding an affordable retreat would be a challenge. I began asking friends for ideas and within a couple of weeks, a door opened. My friend Randy knew someone with a little condo that was nestled between the jungle and the Pacific Ocean in a remote part of Costa Rica, just north of the equator. Having no experience with Central America, I had no idea what to expect. All I knew was that it was far away, the locals spoke Spanish, and it was a relatively friendly destination for U.S. citizens. It was during the hot, dry season, so I was able to rent the place for three months at about the same cost as a single week at a Disney resort.

At this point, what the naysayers in my life thought no longer influenced my decision-making. They worried it would be unsafe, they were concerned I'd lost my mind, and they felt a Disney cruise would be a much wiser getaway. "Bless her heart, she's going off to this God-forsaken place in the jungle ..."

I thanked them for caring about me and assured them I would be available via email. I reminded them that I had thought through the worst possible scenarios that could happen and, while I didn't want misfortune, I would be absolutely OK if they occurred. I excitedly mailed a check to the condo owner and began to get my financial affairs, pet sitters, and travel arrangements in order. The owner arranged for a driver named Léo to meet me at the airport, warning it was not a drive I'd want to attempt without experience.

Once I'd committed to this decision, I felt like I'd kicked open that door from my daydream and stepped outside into a sunny day so blindingly bright that I didn't know what was ahead of me, yet I felt giddy amidst the light. I felt free for the first time in decades. I had no job, I'd given away most of my things, my true friends understood, and both sons were doing well in their respective cities far away.

My childlike curiosity had been reignited. I wanted to grow spiritually, to reconnect with that energy I felt as a kid when riding my horse, exploring the woods, or entertaining congregations with a boogie-woogie-style hymn—that deeply satisfied feeling of joy and freedom I felt at Grandma's house. It occurred to me why we interchange the words "energy" and "power" so easily. They don't have the same definition, but experiencing our energy fully gives us unbridled natural power.

A shift was occurring from pleasing the outside world to listening within. *What sort of potential is hidden inside of me that I've neglected? What powers are already there, and how do I tap into them?* Three weeks later, I left home ready to acknowledge my previous life and shed my skin, to live within and savor every moment of the present, and to gain clarity about my future. I smooched my pets one last time, called my parents to reassure them not to worry, and with one large red suitcase, a trusty backpack, my supplies for journaling, and a phone number for Léo, I set off for the Nashville airport.

PART 2
Tuning In

Welcoming Committee

CHAPTER 9

Welcome to Guiones

Ants: The Native American Hopi Tribe celebrate the ancient Anu-naki, or "ant friends" legend annually. According to cave drawings and long-held tradition, the ant friends welcomed the Hopi into fortified caverns as they fled severe environmental conditions. They taught the Hopi to flourish by remaining below the surface for a period of time while they learned new ways to sustain nourishment with very little water.

Upon arriving at Liberia International Airport in Costa Rica, the 100-degree heat and my driver met me just outside the airport door. My new life had begun. Luggage loaded and windows down, the two-and-a-half-hour drive to Guiones was like riding an exhilarating yet terrifying thrill ride at a pop-up carnival. You're strapped powerlessly in the seat—shocked with each jolt of motion and sickened by the thought of the rickety ride slipping off the rails. Léo spoke no English and swerved past slower vehicles like a long-tailed cat in a room full of rocking chairs. There were no designated lanes, so he just drove on the wrong side of the road as if nothing but his vehicle could possibly occupy the opposing side.

Outside the city, bridges were one lane only. We whizzed past horses, cattle, school children, families on motorcycles, and large semitrucks. Léo stopped halfway for fuel. I scooted across the sticky seats and set off to the outhouse behind the station to pee and puke —in that order. Meanwhile, he purchased two pipas frias, cold coconuts with a hole chopped into the top, and generously offered me one. My body welcomed the sweet, cold water from inside the fruit. Feeling better, I tried out some handy Spanish conversation starters learned in 10th grade and refreshed during the flight. Léo graciously accommodated, discussing apples, the weather, and dogs—prominent topics for beginners in the Duolingo language learning app. Unable to converse beyond my childlike prompts, we fell silent and my gaze skipped among the occasional shanty, the dry rolling hills, and the clusters of small, rustic buildings with colorful hand-painted signs.

Finally, "Guiones 20 KM" on a road sign came into view. From that point on, any sense of familiar infrastructure fell away, replaced by a wild and fascinating landscape. I had expected to see the ocean, but the roads leading down the coast require driving through rivers and often impassable terrain. Instead, there were a lot of trees, cleared plains with bony cattle, and pops of steep hills in the distance. Rugged roads of dirt and gravel were peppered with potholes the size of bathtubs. Feeling like a 92-year-old with merry-go-round motion sickness from the ride, I finally arrived safely at the condo, where I was greeted by Ed, an athletic thirtysomething realtor from New York. He originally visited this area of Costa Rica for its world-class surfing and decided to stay to leverage the emerging housing market. The condo owner paid him an extra 100 bucks to greet me with door keys and drive me to dinner from the remote location.

Ed was dressed in a snug-fitting royal blue t-shirt and dusty cargo shorts. He politely helped me into the condo, and informed me apologetically that he had a hangover from the prior night's revelry and was not in the best of moods. Before we took off to grab dinner, I hopped on my laptop to signal to my family that I had safely made the journey. Confounded by the screen's lack of any sort of signal, I mentioned to Ed that the Wi-Fi was not working. With a knowing chuckle, he replied, "Don't expect cell phone or Wi-Fi from inside of these downstairs condos. I used to live here, and it is like being inside a cave—no signals can reach inside."

Was he kidding?! No phone service in the home? How would I research restaurants in this area? Connect with people from home? Find a new job while on this self-imposed hiatus from corporate life? A sick feeling crept into my gut … *What if there was an emergency way out here in the middle of nowhere?* I wanted time alone in the wilderness, but not solitary confinement. The little voice of the Should Monster inside mocked, *You should be careful what you wish for!*

Ed drove us to Guiones for a quick meal. Along the parched dirt road, I noticed cattle grazing on dry, prickly leftovers from what must have been grass many months ago. Not like the cows from home, these had tall, U-shaped horns and long, droopy ears. Their ribs protruded beneath skin so dusty that when the wind blew, swirling clouds of dirt arose from each skinny bovine frame. Rows of tiny trees served as fence posts, and despite the drought, ruffly pink-petaled pompoms adorned trees in the fields. Ed said they only bloomed during the dry season and locals called them the "Roble de Sabana," meaning "Savannah Oak." Despite my exhaustion, the beauty reminded me that sometimes the harshest conditions provide opportunities to blossom into something extraordinary.

It was March and no rain had fallen since November. Layers of soil were unsettled by a gust of wind near a tiny, open-air home, where chickens pecked about the hut. Ed said chickens eat insects and scorpions, so nearly all rural families welcomed them. As we drove, I tried to make mental notes of the area's landmarks, so I could find my way back to town the following day without access to Google Maps. There wasn't even an address or mailbox for the condo, which should have been my first clue that it was remote beyond anything I had previously experienced. This fact made me feel both excited and a bit nervous.

Edgy Ed and I grabbed an early dinner at the only place that seemed to be serving food at 4:30 p.m. Like most local restaurants, this one was an open-air eatery with the kitchen and bar area anchoring the only solid wall. We pulled up our white plastic chairs at the timeworn wooden table, and I ordered a pineapple-coconut smoothie. The cold drink hit the spot as we chatted about getting around the area. Fast food wasn't a thing in

Guiones. It was always made fresh to order, so it took time. And there weren't any chain restaurants in the little village, so it was easy to shop local. I chose snapper with pineapple salsa, which came with rice and black beans, the most common sides on the hand written menu. I was really going to enjoy eating on this trip.

After dinner, Ed rallied his energy to drop me back at the condo. By this time, it was dark outside. The little condo had a musty odor and a vacant feel, with the exception of a great assortment of ants that propagated the kitchen when the sun went down. The ants were everywhere. And tiny, crawling mite-like bugs. Big ants. Tiny ants. Mites. Everywhere.

Before leaving, Ed said, "Shake out anything left on the floor, because scorpions like hanging out in shoes, towels, or other snuggly places."

"Like inside the bed sheets?"

"Yes. Remember to put lime juice on a scorpion sting—you won't die, it just hurts a lot." *Where were those chickens when I needed them?* "One last thing," he advised. "If you don't know what to say, just say 'Pura Vida.' It means lots of positive things, like 'You're welcome.' 'This is the life!' and 'Have a great day!'"

No bathtub. It would be hard not taking a bath for a few months. Shower only. It was finally time for a steaming hot shower after a long day of travel and luckily the hot water worked. I found myself surprised to realize tears were streaming down my cheeks amidst the soothing water. I'm not sure if they resulted from the unexpected accommodations, the exhausting journey, or the first true exhale of completely disconnecting. The lifetime of purposeful busyness that kept me afloat was also a deceptive salve that masked pain so proficiently it was nearly invisible to me and those closest to me. I tried to remember the last time tears had actually trickled down my cheeks but could not. Each one carried a bit of anxiety, a little frustration, and a little relief.

This fervid pace had been carefully created and maintained to render emotional experiences nearly impossible. It was more efficient to sort and manage the uncontrollable onslaught of setbacks quickly than to risk allowing myself to feel and process them. God knows there was no time to get hung up on my feelings when so many things needed attention. Slowing the pace would have meant inconvenience, ineffectiveness, mediocrity, or heaven forbid, a missed deadline. At home, the boys wouldn't receive the attention they should, and who would pay the bills?

My spouse had struggled to find his purpose after his father passed away and decided not to go back to the type of dependable job he had when we first married. Over the years, he tried a couple of small business ventures that required capital to establish and maintain, so the pressure was on me to provide the steady paycheck, health insurance, and retirement allocations. From the audience of neighbors, colleagues, and family members, it felt like if I allowed peeks beneath the veneer of this perfect family, then they surely would have seen failure.

I reckoned if I got away far enough and long enough to allow time to ponder my past, then perhaps clarity about the future would emerge. Maybe I would be capable of opening my heart to feel again. Refreshed from the hot shower and grateful to be starting the first night of my self-imposed hiatus, the thought that occurred to me as I climbed into bed was: *Well, this is just great. Here you are, thousands of miles from everything and everyone—alone. And yet what was, what is, and what will be are exactly the same in Guiones as they were at home. Dumbass, it's time to stop running.*

Dozens of painful, repressed memories crept into bed beside me each begging for my attention. Unlike the Should Monster, these memories weren't here to haunt or taunt, these were *my* feelings about the past experiences that had been locked away and ignored. The weight of pain in my chest felt so heavy that even breathing took effort. The feelings were real, and they needed me to just sit alongside. Tears began to roll down my cheeks like the heartache was a dam breaking. The experiences that caused the emotional turmoil were finished and now in the rearview mirror. But, as my memories snuggled closer, I thought about the safety warning printed on the passenger side of all motor vehicles, "Objects in mirror are closer than they appear." If the aim was to feel again, this was a long overdue acknowledgement and a successful beginning of the next chapter—successful because it hurt. And I felt it. As the pain of the memories weighed heavy on my heart, my mind clung to its usual coping mechanisms, racing toward something for me to worry about or solve. They kept coming, one after another. Random memories from childhood, like when my parents were talking about a family friend's teenage daughter who was pregnant, and I wondered aloud, "Will you still love me if I get pregnant like Mr. Smith's daughter did when I'm in high school?"

The answer came quickly and without deliberation from my father, "Just don't get pregnant."

"But will you still love me if I mess up?" I inquired, seeking reassurance.

"I said, don't mess up." His words came in that tone that means it would be wise not to ask again, so I nodded that the message had been received.

Another memory poked its head out from under the covers: When in high school after a long day at summer camp, I finished washing my face and turned to rejoin the others sharing our sleeping quarters. One of the beautiful blonde girls from the cheerleading squad smirked in disbelief to the other girls and said to me, "How could *anyone* think you're pretty? Your face is just. So. Ugly." The other girls tried to smooth it over, so she clarified, "Well, it's true. I'm just saying you look a lot better with makeup *on*."

It was like I'd forgotten to put the lid on top of the popcorn popper and random memories were popping up and flying everywhere. Like the statement overheard from a colleague referring to my ability to secure a large financial contract with the federal government at such a young age and with a small company: "I'm sure she just slept her way into it. Nobody's gonna give that kind of money to somebody like that unless she earned it the 'old fashioned' way."

To escape, I diverted my thoughts back to the present to all the bugs and the 1,000 scorpions that must be patiently forming a military coup under the bed, just waiting for me to step over the edge without looking first. Before leaving Nashville, I thought mosquitoes would be the only bug issue, so I brought geranium oil and put it across the threshold of my bedroom because my friend Kim promised it was a natural mosquito repellent. *Perhaps it would work for ants, mites, spiders, and scorpions too?* I itched at the thought of crawly critters everywhere, but they were inescapable, so I resolved to live peacefully with them.

I brought my journal in the bed with me. I wanted to record the events of my first day while they were fresh in my mind. The random, pop-up memories caused more tears to gently fall. As mites and ants dotted across the papers upon which I was writing, they carefully avoided the tiny puddles of tear droplets, so I resisted the urge to smash them. As long as they were not biting, I vowed to embrace the little fellas as my welcoming committee. All living things serve an important purpose.

Tunnel in Arenal Skybridge Park

CHAPTER 10

Off to a Rocky Start

Peak-to-Peak Amplitude: The change between a peak and its corresponding trough. Each is a peak in its own direction, but one represents the highest point and the other represents the lowest point.

Morning made its entrance through the broken bamboo blinds after a night of vivid dreams. I rarely took time to record them in the past unless they seemed extraordinary but committed to pen them every day while in Costa Rica. One of the dreams was a clear vision of the words "Guilo Roberto" on a plain piece of paper. I had no idea what it meant but scribed it, nonetheless, alongside the other intriguing scenes remaining in short-term memory. It was the start of my big adventure in the wilderness, so I eagerly headed to town with transportation and communication needs in my head and excitement in my heart. It felt like being a kid again, face to the wind, headed into the open air on my horse, Betty. Nature is always alive with energy.

I began walking to town and made it about a mile before Ed drove by in his dusty dark blue Toyota 4Runner. He stopped to pick me up. It was perfect timing, because two large dogs had just noticed me, and I realized I left the pepper spray back at the condo. One dog was a thin, tall fellow with wiry hair. The other looked like a bony German shepherd mixed with a Lab. I decided to call them Abbott and Costello. *Note to self: You look like a tasty cheeseburger to the hungry dogs that live in the woods between your condo and the road to town. Another note to self: Always bring the pepper spray.*

I found a surprising little place in the tiny village called Café de Paris. It served breakfast and offered Wi-Fi, so I sent a few messages home to let everyone know I made it safely. The smoothies were offered in precisely 32 different ways. This time, I tried mango and ordered the French toast, expecting the syrup laden hunks of thick bread like we made at home. Instead, the toast was made with sweet bread, poached corn, honey, and mint, which sounds a bit odd but was the perfect complement to my fruity drink.

I spent a few hours investigating the businesses along the main roadway and exploring the village's footpaths used by locals, or "ticos" (men) and "ticas" (women). Along the winding jungle path, giant trees boasted thick buttress roots—huge exposed root systems that looked like giant octopus tentacles twisting and plunging into the forest floor. Large iguanas and little lizards scampered across the crinkly leaves underfoot. One path led to a luxury yoga resort built in the treetops overlooking the beach. Another path led to a magnificent collection of giant black rocks that formed cliffs by the water's edge. There was a network of ancient paths connecting the four main destinations in the little town. It was beautiful, quiet, peaceful, and exotic.

The local bicycle shop offered bike rentals for the discounted rate of $50 a day. For a few months, that came to thousands of dollars—far more than I planned to spend on transportation. I asked how much it would cost to buy a new bike like ones they rented. The cycling shop employee looked at me as if I'd asked something completely outlandish, then replied, "We would have to charge $187." In her mind, that was much more expensive than $50 a day, so I quickly agreed to the price. Thankfully, I had become the proud new owner of a bright blue leisure-style bicycle that looked like something from the 1950s.

Before leaving, I noticed a brochure on the checkout counter about mountain-biking trails and asked the clerk if she knew of any hiking trails.

She did not, but an American man in the store overheard me and spoke up. He introduced himself, but it was muffled so I didn't catch his name. He had the brightest blue eyes and a kind, captivating way of speaking. The man said he ran to and from work each day but was not aware of local off-road recreational trails. I gave him my old business card with a personal email address scribbled on it and said if he heard of any that would be safe for a directionally challenged foreigner to traverse alone to send them to me.

Within a few minutes, I learned that riding an old-fashioned bicycle on the raggedy dirt roads with drivers of all types whizzing by was like playing life-sized dodgeball with motorcycles and trucks. Luckily, I packed a long-sleeved lightweight white shirt. The day reached a sweltering 100 degrees again, and *dry* doesn't begin to describe how parched the ground was. Each passing vehicle produced a miniature dust storm, leaving me covered with caked-on layers of dirt and in dire need of Visine. The shirt provided a little protection from each dust tsunami and quickly became my favorite (brown) item of clothing.

On the way home, I picked up a few groceries at the local store. They didn't have any spaghetti sauce, just ketchup and pasta. I don't like ketchup, so I purchased:

1 box of noodles

1 bag of coffee

2 potatoes

1 large bag of oatmeal

1 pot with lid (There were no cooking items at the condo.)

2 types of butter (I was not sure which was margarine; I didn't get that far along in the Spanish Duolingo app.)

1 carton of orange-carrot juice (which I thought was regular orange juice until I drank the first glass)

3 yogurt drinks (to pour over cereal brought from home)

I also tried to buy some Parmesan cheese, but the cashier showed me it was out of date, so he put it back (yep, on the shelf).

Once I got back to my bicycle, the ticos standing outside the store were clearly wondering, "How's that gringa going to carry all that on the bike?" I wondered that, too, but didn't let them see me sweat. After all, Kentucky-born women are strong and tough! I put some things in the pot, which I placed in the front basket, and tied other items into a bag on the back fender. Strapped into my trusty backpack—which was already full with my laptop, purse, water bottle, and brochures and pamphlets from the village—off I awkwardly peddled, barely able to balance the heavy weight on the rocky dirt road. And the clanging began. It was as if there was a monkey on my handlebars crashing cymbals together—the pot and its lid were the culprit.

Regardless of pulling over and packing, repacking, putting items between the lid and pot, as well as cussing a good bit under my breath, there was no way to avoid the loud "clingity-clang." The bumpy dirt road kept jostling things around, so the crashing-pot alarm resumed. Like a bag-lady cyclist, I had too many groceries, turtle-dirty skin, and was on a goofy leisure bicycle instead of a motorbike like any reasonably intelligent person. Excited for the adventure and chalking it up to a rookie mistake, I focused on driving sideways through the pothole-like ruts to prevent going head over handlebars.

Things were moving along well until I reached the lane that led to the little condo. A growing panic emerged as I remembered Abbott and Costello. The clanging would surely draw their attention. With a fully loaded bike, how would I out-pedal them? I had built up momentum. But with a load packed high like the Grinch's sled in *How the Grinch Stole Christmas,* Lord knows I could *not* stop without tipping over. Maybe the dogs would smell the groceries and try to get to them? Maybe they would settle for my shoes if I could wiggle out of them on the fly. Bargaining tactics raced through my mind as I decided the best strategy was to keep going as fast as safely possible in the hope that they would get tired or go for the butter—or the margarine.

Luckily for me, the cow across from the woods where the dogs lived was giving birth, so the locals were out in the street watching. It was a huge relief Abbott and Costello were temporarily clocked out from guard duty. I smiled broadly at the neighbors from atop my very noisy bike. "Hola!" They smiled back as their heads followed me *all the way* down the lane. The condo was just over the next hill. The slick street bicycle tires spun mercilessly in the loose, dry sediment as I peddled hard to keep from falling over. My racing heart rang loudly in my ears, but not as loudly as the pot. *This surely counts as a workout,* I thought.

Grateful to be "home," I dismounted the bicycle and noticed men digging a large hole in the front yard of the condo. They were speaking English, so I asked what was going on. Someone had backed over the water main and broken the pipe—there would be *no water* until they could repair it. They aimed to have it fixed by next week. While the news sank in, I took my groceries—and trusty new bike—inside to unload. Thank God for orange-carrot juice.

I changed into a swimsuit then put shampoo and soap all over my dirt-caked body. At this point, I pretended it was an exotic mud-pack treatment at the spa rather than dirt, shampoo, and soap smothering every square inch. Looking first out the window and then peeking around the abandoned upstairs condos near the pool, I checked for signs of humans. With no one around, this was my chance to use the pool as an interim bathtub. While it wasn't ideal for me, or the cleanliness of the pool water given the dirt roads and amount of grime I inhaled throughout the day, finding some way to wash up was the *only* option. The sun fell as I emerged chlorine-clean and slinked down the steps to sneak back inside.

The ants scurried a wiggly "hello" when the lights turned on. I cooked up noodles with butter-margarine and pulled up my heaping plate alongside the welcoming committee. My first full day in Costa Rica was over and with its end, fear of the past began to settle, and awareness of and great gratitude for the present started to emerge. There was no place I needed to be; no TV, no Wi-Fi, or cell service; no alarm required. Nobody was depending on me to fix something, yelling at me, mocking me, or expecting anything productive from me. I felt like I was walking through a dark tunnel and being able to see something beautiful at its end, as if I would soon emerge into a new world.

Cows in road between Guiones and Nicoya

CHAPTER 11

Big Wheels

Potential Energy: Energy with the potential to be converted into other forms. It may also refer to other forms of stored-up energy, such as internal stresses. Potential energy is defined in equations by the letter U.

Day two of my adventure in Guiones had begun. It was apparent using a bicycle on those roads long-term was a death wish and exploring beyond a few miles at a time was not feasible. I was 0 for 2 at the first two car places. Cars everywhere were already sold out, because apparently this was high tourist season in the nearby surf village of Nosara. I peddled my trusty, dusty bicycle into the third and final option for a rental car, a place called Limo Dan's.

I introduced myself to Limo Dan with a tired smile and the best hopes of talking him into at least a golf-cart rental. Dan was a former competitive athlete from Dallas who moved his limo service to Costa Rica after visiting years ago. He was a tall, toned, and confident man with dark, wavy hair and an impossibly white smile. I noticed a tattoo inside his left bicep "Porque no?"—which roughly translates into "Why not?"—and resisted the urge to ask about it. I had a hunch this was the kind of guy who had a deep reservoir of interesting stories, the kind who would gladly share them after a few beers.

I tried some random chit-chatty conversation, hoping to build on our bond of being Americans, but Limo Dan assured me no cars would be available until after Easter weekend, which was more than a month away. After learning I'd be his neighbor out the rural little road in Guiones, however, he took a bit of pity and said to come back on April 17th and he would give me a good deal for the remainder of my visit. It was strike 3 on getting a car, but I was happy to have met someone who lived nearby.

Until then, I was bicycle-bound, which also meant being back at the condo in the afternoon. It was too dangerous to cycle after dark. There were no streetlights, and even when I rigged the iPhone flashlight to my bicycle basket, the risk of waking up Abbott and Costello was too great. I imagined them sitting upright on their doggie bums at a table for two, both gnawing hungrily on my calves (one for each of them) like hungry lumberjacks at Thanksgiving dinner. Dan gave me the number to reach the driver of a three-wheeled open-air "tuk-tuk," except I didn't have any way to call a driver without a working phone. Yet.

So, the next step was to visit the only store in town large enough to sell phone SIM cards. Turns out if you have a Verizon phone, it is often locked so you cannot use local SIM cards. The store owner explained that my phone was worthless here. I would need to buy another phone, which could hopefully be done in the nearest town, about 10 miles away. With only a bicycle, and with rocky dirt roads, that would be a couple hours' pedaling in each direction. There were no local maps of this part of Costa Rica, only a hand-drawn picture map I picked up at the bicycle shop. Upon arriving in the nearby town, it would then require deducing where to go. I blinked back the annoying tears of frustration that threatened to well up as he informed me of my bleak options for communicating whilst in Guiones. Unless I was in a restaurant that provided Wi-Fi, there would be no connecting.

Why was I so perturbed? After all, I loved long, quiet hikes in the wilderness, but those were usually with a friend or guide. I realized not only was I alone—with my newfound feelings—but I was stripped of the freedom a vehicle allows and the productivity and connection that a phone fosters. All the movement, chatter, and checking of to-do list boxes that was my comfort zone were gone. This was the original intent, but who knew it would be *this* isolated?

Being alone with the voices in my head felt uncomfortable, like when your sock is too big and it keeps scrunching down into your shoe. Wrinkles of awkwardness form under your foot, and you have to consciously make the decision whether to take the time and smooth it out or to continue forward nonetheless, aware with each step of the discomfort. I decided to let my proverbial sock remain where it was rather than where it "should" be and dug deep for toughness: *Stay positive. You called out to the universe for direction, and the powerful answers brought you here. This is your journey, including the speed bumps and roadblocks—so be in the moment and lean into it!* I viewed the challenges as little adventures. After all, I wouldn't *die* without a phone and a car. It was like being a kid again, exploring in the woods.

I found a spot with Wi-Fi to email a couple distress signals. The first was to a friend from Nashville, Wayne, who was making a documentary film a few hours north of my location in Costa Rica at the time. Wayne was a fellow champion for the environment and a successful businessman with a big heart. I shared the challenges of getting transportation in my part of the country and asked if he had any ideas where I may find an inexpensive car to rent 'til mid-April. Then I emailed Randy, my friend who connected me with the condo owner. He had offered numerous times before I left to send me a package if I got to the foreign village and needed anything. I asked him to send ant traps, sunscreen, eye drops, and spaghetti sauce. Then I said goodbye to Wi-Fi and cycled back to the condo.

Upon reaching my temporary home, I reminded myself that although things were not turning out the way they had played out in my imagination, I was safe and healthy, and I had completed another step towards finding it. Who knew what "it" was, but I was determined to shed my skin and find it while in Costa Rica.

On the third day, I continued the routine of morning cereal and coffee with the ants, then headed to the little village to explore and check messages. New emails were waiting in the inbox when I opened my laptop at a lunch spot with Wi-Fi. Wayne had arranged for me to pick up a rental car in the northern part of the country for the next month at $942, with insurance included. By the time I got this message, he was already driving to my location. Wayne looked up a restaurant online and told me he'd pick me up there but was uncertain how long it would take him to navigate the dirt roads and river crossings—some without bridges. So, I headed to the rendezvous point, and a couple hours later, he arrived like a fabulous knight in a dusty white 4x4. Securing a reliable means of transportation was becoming a reality, and my heart swelled at the thought. Having a car would allow me to more safely explore and stay out past mid-afternoon.

We drove over an hour to Nicoya where there were paved roads, schools, churches, and commercial businesses. The bustling little city had clothing shops, electronic stores, and small restaurants called "sodas" that served mostly a choice of meat and two sides—rice and black beans or a salad. We stopped at a place that was like a cross between an American big-box retailer and a local flea market. I bought a little phone with prepaid time on it. Then we drove further north, just outside of Nicoya, where the car rental representative was waiting at a KFC restaurant. It was the only chain restaurant I had seen outside of Liberia, the city hosting the country's northern national airport. I was abundantly happy to have a car—and mashed potatoes with gravy.

Wayne was the most tech-savvy Baby Boomer I had ever met. He was using Google Translate to talk with the store clerks who spoke no English, using the Waze app to navigate around the countryside, and had to break briefly for a Skype chat with the Harpeth River Watershed team back home. A very kind man, he invited me to an event the Costa Rican nonprofit he was working with was hosting the following Saturday in Junquillal, so I made a mental note to go and support the fundraising efforts. It was the least I could do in return for his many kindnesses.

My mind was more at ease having a sedan to safely navigate the area, and Wayne lent me his old GPS system to use in the rental car. He warned to never leave it in the car unattended and asked me to bring it back home to Nashville afterwards, so I happily accepted the loan. Although the condo where I was staying did not have a street address, the GPS was an absolute lifesaver to get me to the closest village. The 90-minute drive back from Nicoya was mostly paved for the first half, but it turned into a real adventure for the last half of the drive. It may seem odd, but going from a world of comfort in the U.S. to unpaved, unmarked terrain was exhilarating. The surroundings echoed a simplicity and peace that had lain dormant in me since childhood.

The remaining road back to the condo was an obstacle course augmented by my stick-shift-driving skills, which had been unused since high school. The journey consisted of dirt, gravel, and pothole-filled roads; a herd of goats and then a herd of cows ambling lazily down the middle of the road; a dusty gravel incline that nearly killed me because I kept stalling out the engine; one-lane bridges; blind hills; and gung-ho pedestrians, motorcycles, and semitrucks. I never knew what would be just around the bend. It was a free-for-all road adventure that left me feeling like I had experienced a cross between the demolition derby at the county fair and an old-fashioned game of chicken.

Back in the condo at the end of a challenging yet invigorating day, I washed my filthy face and checked out my reflection in the mirror. While the drought caused dehydration, dry eyes, and crusty turtle skin, it made for amazing hair. I momentarily considered starting dreadlocks. Given the condo's community of crawling friends, the inescapable dirt, and occasional lack of running water, I resolved that in Costa Rica, there would be no makeup and no fiddling with hairdos.

It felt great to take a break from caring about looks or perceptions, another "should" I could shed here. At what point did it seem like a good idea for women to go to extensive lengths to color our hair, paint our faces and nails, and contort our bodies into uncomfortable clothes and shoes all in the name of beauty? Many of us feel compelled to spend twice the amount of time on our appearances as men to make ourselves presentable, and we do our best to emulate the airbrushed, unrealistic examples surrounding us in print and online ... just another sly way the Should Monster maneuvers his way into our minds.

I lay in bed that night trying to blink, but there was not enough moisture in my eyes. I could *hear* my eyelids trying to close completely, which in equal parts fascinated and horrified me. I felt good, though, because this day marked the end of the needs portion of my trip. I had big enough wheels to get around, food, shelter, and a phone I would soon connect. It would be all downhill from here.

Baby Sea Turtles

CHAPTER 12

Go with the Flow

Newton's First Law of Motion: An object in motion will remain in motion (in the absence of an unbalanced force).

With day four in front of me, there was no set itinerary, no schedule, no deadlines, only a feeling of anticipation and excitement for adventure. Kickstarting the day with a full-on fancy-free attitude, I decided to visit Playa Ostional—one of the largest turtle-hatching areas in the world. I imagined a beautiful drive through the unexplored countryside, then emerging upon a beach full of sweet baby turtles. With renewed optimism, I hopped in my weather-worn sky-blue sedan and set off with a high-level country map to Ostional. I couldn't wait to pop up the 15 miles or so to witness sea turtles all around me. I would take lots of photos and try to hug each and every one.

I decided to take a quick detour to check out Nosara proper first, though. Evidently, I didn't turn quickly enough and ended up on a 40-minute one-lane dirt-road loop. I chalked it up to a scenic detour through the countryside and made a mental note to turn earlier next time. Upon making it back to the main road, I followed the signs to Playa Ostional. There were several blind, one-lane bridges along the way. Vehicles had to drive up onto the platform to see if anyone was coming from the other direction. That was not the most frightening encounter, however. That came later when the only road dipped down into a muddy creek. You couldn't tell if the water was one or seven feet deep.

I was nervous beyond belief and put on my emergency flashers to evaluate next steps. A small SUV passed me and went through the creek. Then another SUV went through it at an angle. I decided I would try driving through it at the same angle and hope for the best. I had driven this far, so what was the worst thing that could happen? I remembered to bring along pepper spray for any wayward dogs, plus there were homes about a half-mile back that I could walk to if it didn't work out. Surely one of the homes would have a working phone I could borrow, so I mentally thought through calling the car rental agency to explain what had happened and find out what to do next: *Um…sí…Habla inglés? Gracias! I'm terribly sorry, but I've managed to run your car into a creek. What should we do about that?*

With a deep breath I said aloud, "Ready, set, go." I went. My tiny sedan and I made it and my heart resumed its normal rhythm. After all, according to the trusty GPS, I was only 2 kilometers from the turtles I would hug to bits and love forever. In about 15 minutes, I came upon a soda diner and a liquor store with a man outside who looked at me like I was in the wrong place. There was also a tiny abandoned church. This was indeed Playa Ostional. I had arrived. I drove further to make sure I hadn't missed the "See Turtles Here" signs.

I drove back and parked by the beach at the soda, then hopped out and eagerly combed the beach for turtles, but it was empty except for a few locals eating lunch under a shade structure. It was 98 degrees and had taken me 90 minutes to get this far (given my detour around Nosara), so I decided to head inside and grab a bite to eat and some cold water. "Habla inglés?" I asked.

"No," the woman behind the counter promptly replied and handed me a menu. I looked at the menu and ordered pollo con salsa, chicken in sauce. It came with the traditional rice, black beans, and a salad. It was delicious. All the meals thus far in Costa Rica had been fresh and tasty. What was an imported treat in Nashville, like fresh mangos, literally dropped from trees alongside the road here like walnuts or acorns did back home. An endless supply of tropical fruits and fresh fish from the Pacific was the staple diet.

As for drinks, however, wine wasn't the easiest commodity to find in the rural areas. The supermarkets were often open air with high heat, so conditions weren't ideal for storing wine. Never having acquired a taste for beer, I learned there were basically two brands of "cerveza" sold at most restaurants, Imperial and Pilsen. If the day was especially arduous, I chose an Imperial. Not because I appreciated its taste, but because it had a cool-looking dragon on the bottle.

I used *el baño* (the toilet) before leaving—I couldn't hold it any longer. The restroom was a little shack in a lean-to outside the soda with a hole in the floor, which worked out just fine because it provided all the necessities. It wasn't the appearance of the toilet that was unnerving, it was the realization that there was very little privacy. This echo chamber seemed to amplify my bathroom activity like an unorthodox concert playing from a loudspeaker, a symphony of the tinkling triangle singing forth from the primitive pit accentuated by tuba-like bean-induced toots. I was certain the guy outside the liquor store heard it. I reckoned everybody has to go eventually, so I soldiered on with my most confident smile upon leaving the squatty-potty. "Pura vida" flowed off my tongue. *Maybe he thought I was a local.*

Before driving back to the condo, I took one last scan of the beach. I found a tiny area like a chicken coop with a few handmade signs on it that meant "Here is where we incubate the turtle eggs." Nobody was around. Definitely no turtle life. Disappointed, I headed home. I would later learn there are very specific days that correspond with tides when the turtles hatch. *Note to self: must come back to experience that on another trip in the future.*

As I approached the river pit on the drive back, another tourist in a small SUV stopped at the creek's edge in front of me and got out of his car. I put down the window and asserted, "Hey man, just drive sideways towards that direction, you'll make it, no problem. It's fine!" Clearly, I had become a local expert on driving through rivers. He took my word for it and drove through. I followed him back through the water and then took a right towards Guiones over the one-way bridge, or "rasta," named by the locals for its Rastafarian-themed red, green, gold, and black pillars.

Upon passing a restaurant in town that had Wi-Fi, I pulled off the road close enough to get a signal and check messages. Waiting in my inbox was a short email from the American in the bicycle shop whom I had asked about hiking trails. His name was Rob and he invited me to join him and a couple of his colleagues at Olga's Bar at Playa Pelada at sunset, a local tradition. This was my chance to meet some locals, and since it was already late afternoon, I decided to stop by and give it a try before heading back to the condo. *What time is sunset?* I wondered. Olga's was about a mile up a winding dirt road. Million-dollar homes and shanties alike dotted the hillsides on the way up to this little restaurant.

Once I got there, I met Rob and his friend, Brian, from work. They built homes and small commercial buildings locally. We took in the gorgeous view of the sun setting over the mighty roaring Pacific—breathtaking! Rob did not have a car yet or a phone that worked without Wi-Fi either. He reminded me that he ran or cycled, using a proper mountain bike, the 6 miles to and from his job each day, so surely between us we could find some off-road trails. Rob was a psychologist originally from Washington state who most recently lived in Montana, then Alaska, before coming to Guiones to help his childhood friend, Brian. He grew up the son of a tailor, and his family made custom clothing. He had been in Costa Rica since November building small hotels, custom homes, and commercial spaces. He looked like an older version of Brad Pitt but with silver hair, a thin runner's build, and bright blue eyes. He was shy, respectful, and intelligent. He shared some of his Costa Rica stories and tips for a newbie like me.

These were his key takeaways:

He stepped on a large snake one night when walking home, so always use a flashlight because some snakes come out at night.

He reinforced that I would definitely encounter a scorpion at some point, so don't freak out, just put lime juice on the sting.

He advised getting used to the biting ants—over time, your body acclimates, and it would not hurt anymore.

We grabbed food at an open-air Italian restaurant next door to Olga's. Rob cycled home in the dark afterwards, and I attempted to drive home without using the GPS. After ending up at a dead end with raging guard dogs jumping onto my car, my heart pounding, I decided it would be a lovely idea to turn on the guidance system to navigate back to the main road. It felt great to have a car—and a GPS. The day had flown by in the blink of an eye, and I felt my journey shifting from inertia to forward momentum.

Upon arriving home that evening, I noticed the words written from my first night's dream, "Guilo Roberto." I would later learn that "Guilo" means "white man or Westerner" in one language and "tailor" in another. "Roberto" is Spanish for "Robert." It was an eerie but cool affirmation to realize that I met a white man who was a tailor named Robert, after seeing those words in my dream and writing them down. I thanked God for communicating so plainly with me—His way of saying the Spirit was and would be with me during my journey.

I was beginning to tap more directly into my intuition, and I vowed to not only continue keeping a dream journal every night during the trip, but also to keep bravely exploring the unfamiliar. Each day of venturing out and taking new risks—whether driving through rivers, cycling home from the grocery, or trying a new type of fruit smoothie—was rekindling that childlike feeling of freedom, a sense of play where you're so enthralled with creating or exploring, so lost in the fullness of the moment that you completely forget about time and responsibilities. It's joy. But you have to take the risk, to brave a few muddy crossings, wild dogs, or empty baby-sea-turtle beaches to get there.

On Alert

CHAPTER 13

Scorpion Rodeo

Scorpion: An ancient symbol of power, the scorpion represents transformation through death of the old and rebirth into the new. Rebirth could be with the self and others, of ideas and beliefs, or a complete change in one's way of life.

The scorpion dam had broken. Within a 24-hour period, four of them greeted me with a great deal of crankiness, as indicated by their arched tail with barbed stinger erect and ready to strike. The first was behind the toilet (thankfully not *in* the toilet). I coaxed him to a place where I could put a KFC cup over him. He was far too frisky to risk picking the cup up to slide on its lid, so I scooted him across the bathroom and through the bedroom, dodging the suitcase on the floor, into the living room, around the bicycle, and out the front door where I gave him a good fling out onto the hill beyond the front stoop.

I nearly stepped on the second one at 2 a.m. during my middle-of-the-night trip between the bed and toilet. I turned the light on every time I got out of bed at night just in case and am thoroughly glad I did. I'm sorry to say this one was killed. He was scrambling towards me, despite my best 'possum-like hisses to scare him back. I grabbed the DEET insect repellant and sprayed him—to no avail. Panicking a wee bit at this point, I poured bleach on him—again to no avail. He was too fired up to get into

91

a container, so I used the toilet bowl brush to keep pushing him back into the pile of chemicals until he slowed down enough for me to chop him into three pieces and flush them. It all felt a little dramatic and violent, perhaps because it was the middle of the night. I didn't sleep a wink afterwards.

The next day, Rob informed me that killing a scorpion brought bad karma. *Now he tells me!* Sure enough, when I pulled back the covers and raised a leg to climb into bed that evening, there was a third scorpion inside my sheets, just waiting to be lain upon so he could sting me (or perhaps cozy up with me under the covers). I remembered all the self-talk from earlier in the day: *What's the worst thing that happens? They get in my bed and sting me. I would not die ... So I shall agree to let them live and ask that they kindly leave me alone.*

Clearly, the scorpion coup must not have heard the "leave me alone" part of that conversation, because a fourth scorpion lurked in my towel hanging over the shower rod. I found a short plastic container to offer a bit of buffer, since this one was at eye level, and got him into it. The lid would not completely shut because his little stinger tail was sticking out the top. I reasoned with him on the way out the door and over to the grassy hill beyond the driveway, "Now look, little guy, you are going to be happy out here, and you want to stay outside and play with your friends and leave me alone. OK? OK."

Again, I didn't sleep. Not a wink. Every time I started to drift off, the feeling of something under the covers ... *No, on top of them ... Was that a scamper coming down from the AC unit on the wall? No, that sound was the AC unit taking its last breath.* Now, in the middle of the night, I was scared *and* hot. People warned me about the little monsters, but they said I may see *one* while here. The next day, frazzled from a lack of sleep, I learned from a local at a cafe that it is quite rare to run across so many in succession—unheard of, really. I wondered if this, like the snakes, is another sign from what I like to think is my grandma.

Are they a totem representing personal growth? Am I supposed to face some sort of fear? What about me is surrounded by a hard shell for protection? I knew if scorpions were another symbol from beyond, they were by far the most frightening sign yet. With the snakes, I didn't have to worry about checking under the toilet lid or sheets. These little guys were feisty and fast, and they meant business. This wasn't your average Kentucky pet. This was a whole new ballgame and I had to be hyper-aware, vigilant … I had to put my game face on. I decided to utilize all of my resources: I got in touch with the property manager; I resolved to better tune in to my Inner Owl, in case this was a sign that would not go away until I figured it out; and I asked God for a favor.

Dear God, Grandma, and anyone else on this frequency,

Please allow me to find love and peace in my heart for the scorpions, giant spiders, endless ants, mosquitoes, and other biting bugs here. Grant me the strength to stay strong during this journey … to complete what has been started. Help me understand the things of cardinal importance and be willing to stand as an unwavering rock for them. I don't want to be a chicken. Amen.

P.S. You may, however, send a hungry chicken.

The next morning, I swept the floor to tidy up a bit and the property manager, Luis, promised to visit by noon to discuss some scorpion-mitigation strategies. Lo and behold, number five was clinging to the towel I used to cover the gaping crack under the front door. Quite happy that the towel was there, I took him outside. By this point, I was resigned to the fact that "scorpion wrangling" should be added to my list of LinkedIn qualifications. I left number five on what I officially christened "Scorpion Hill."

As the day drew on, my conscience began bothering me about the scorpion I killed. The only thing bigger than a Baptist's fear of being caught buying liquor is her sense of guilt. It must have felt awful to have bleach poured on him, poor little guy. It reminded me of a time as a young adult when we lived on a farm and mice kept getting into the pantry. Someone at work recommended sticky-pad traps, which I naively thought would have a poison that quickly and humanely killed them. I placed a sticky pad on the second pantry shelf from the top, right next to the Cap'n Crunch cereal box, and within a few hours heard tiny terrified little squeals.

I rushed to the pantry and flung open the door in panic to find three baby mice stuck to the pad, their little voices shrieking for help. Horrified, I picked up the pad and began trying to remove them from it, my long frizzy hair connecting solidly as I leaned in. With frenetic fervor I heard the mother of all mice racing up between the walls and nearing the tiny hole on the backside of the pantry shelf. I stood wide-eyed and dumbfounded with an angry mama mouse emerging onto the shelf at eye-level, racing to save her three wailing babies that dangled like an oversized earring under my left ear. Needless to say, it didn't end well.

I called my dad, who lived a few miles away, to take the baby mice out into the field and promise not to tell me what happened next. My conscience bothered me for days. I didn't kill any more mice but did opt for a short haircut the following day.

Luis, the property manager, came a few hours late and used a strong insecticide throughout the condo. The combo of Benadryl, which I took to try to sleep after missing so much rest, plus the potent insecticide fumes must have knocked me out, because I slept through the entire night and into the following day. Feeling refreshed, and likely high from the intense chemicals, I worked with a local woman to clean every square inch of the condo that next afternoon—washing sheets and bedding, floors, bathrooms—if there were any scorpions left hiding, we surely would have found them.

Or not. By the next morning, the sixth and seventh scorpions presented themselves, each different in size, variation of color, and level of belligerence. Upon meeting that lucky seven milestone, I grabbed a large rock and smashed it with furious frustration. To hell with my conscience. I guess it had been smothered by my exhausted patience. It was too many, too soon, and trying to resume normalcy was impossible!

But my intuition began speaking. As with the snakes, I felt there was a message from this highly unusual occurrence. Since scorpions were so foreign and frightening to me, I reasoned it must be about facing something that scared me deeply. But what? I couldn't understand this message. I cleaned up the murdered arachnid, asked him for forgiveness, and dropped his mortal coil in the trash can. Standing in the condo, frustration racing and eyes darting to catch the next little clawed gladiator, the thought crossed my mind to pack up and go back home.

Cardinal Clarity

CHAPTER 14

Cardinal Clarity

Cardinal: [car·di·nal] adj. of the greatest importance; fundamental;
Symbolism: The cardinal represents spiritual
connection and appears in writings as a representative
of departed loved ones or sign of hope.

I drove to the beach and tackled the rocky, steep path I'd fallen on twice earlier that week. It was beautiful, but quite scary, from the top. I went part of the way down the tiny 8-inch-wide ridge-top trail but decided with dangerous drops in each direction, crashing waves beneath, and no one to call for help—there's no 911 in Guiones—I had better wait until someone came along with me before climbing to the very end.

I took this time without distractions to reflect upon what was really important to me, not what would please everyone else. This didn't come naturally to me, and it felt odd. I used the time climbing the cliffs and listening to the rumbling water beneath to consider many life events I hadn't thought about in decades. Initially, I was trying to decide if I should invite one of my guy friends from back home to visit me in Costa Rica. It would allow me to venture along the remote areas more safely, and, who knows—maybe it would lead to something more romantic. Letting men get close had never been easy. My track record seemed to lead from one painful experience to the next, each adding another layer of armor around my heart. That day, I allowed my mind to relive the first part of the series.

At age 17, my best friend Dana and I went to a party out in the country. Upon arrival, she met up with her boyfriend and they left for the night. We were to meet up in the morning and she would take me home. Of course, I deceptively told my parents I'd be staying over with Dana, careful to leave off the part "at her house." I knew enough friends would be at the party, so I planned to sleep in the house. After a drink, I remembered my purse was left lying on the top of the car. This area was a safe, little idyllic country town, plus my friends were only 100 feet away inside the house, so I never gave a second thought to retrieving it in the dark. The last thing I remembered from that night was reaching up to grab the purse and hearing a loud, hollow "thump" like the sound of hitting a watermelon to see if it was ripe, then feeling heat flowing down the back of my head during the cold winter night. I woke up confused and in shock hours later in a nearby ditch.

The Should Monster told me I had been tarnished; I was damaged goods. If I told someone, I'd forever be known as that girl who was attacked—or worse, the girl who "put herself in a situation" where she got raped—instead of the upstanding image I had worked hard to become. I couldn't resolve to even think, much less speak, of that four-letter word so many women endure. Instead, I thought about Dad's words over and over: *There is no such thing as a mistake, only a stupid decision.* I would disappoint my family for being at a party where underage drinking occurred—what kind of example was I being for others?

My brain and heart raced with equal parts shock, sadness, guilt, and of course outright rage for not being given the chance to fight back to at least try to defend myself against the attacker and make him pay for thinking he could harm me without consequence. The Should Monster said I should have done so many things differently and that people would harshly judge me, so I should keep this to myself. It said I should focus on repenting, doing things in the church, and volunteering to make other people happy for God's sake, then maybe He'll forgive me. Surely this was my punishment for sneaking out to a party and deceiving my parents. The Should Monster added that I should suck it up and accept responsibility, that I had sinned and was being punished.

So, I did just that—I began volunteering more with one of the talented, charismatic church elders and a Gospel music vocalist, Jim. We performed at churches in the area, visited nursing homes, even made a gospel tape of our music for the elderly or sick who were unable to attend services in person. I was comfortable around him because of his kindness to others and commitment to the church. So, I didn't think anything unusual when he insisted on taking me to a local restaurant for my 18th birthday.

For weeks, he had been telling me about the dreams he was having and that God was working in his life. He and the woman he had been dating had broken up, but God had a new plan, he said. I was happy for Jim, until he let me know the person God had chosen for him was … me. He was convinced he saw "rings of light" around me as the reinforcing sign. I was to bear him two sons. He had already chosen the names for the boys. He was quite certain of all of this and gave me a card expressing his love, then tried to kiss me.

Rejecting him, he said, would be to deny God's will. Needless to say, I was surprised at this revelation. I got out of the car and walked to our nearby high school where a basketball game was taking place. I caught a ride home with a friend from there. I didn't want any part of this. I told Jim the next Sunday after church that I had always thought he was a kind elder friend, that I would never be with him romantically, and that we should stop volunteering together.

But Jim wouldn't let it go. He was so persistent that he began telling mutual family friends about his dreams. And in the dreams, he now imagined me in a wheelchair because, as he put it, "That is where God will put her, so she realizes how much she needs me." The friends became so concerned for my safety that they told my parents. With my dad's family history of short-tempered brawlers and his extensive gun collection, I can only imagine what he did or said to Jim, but I didn't hear from him the rest of the time I was in high school, and he started attending a different church.

The first year of college was a blur. I worked the night shift as a GTE telephone operator while taking full-time semester loads (15-16 credit hours). This efficiently met the needs of my favorite coping mechanism: Stay so busy you cannot think or, heaven forbid, feel. In the blink of an eye I had completed a year of school and moved about an hour away to finish the degree in Louisville. Whether it was Jim's steady mental decline or the fact that I was, for the first time, away from the safety of my family and friends, suddenly, he began showing up after classes or randomly on the way to school. It happened a few times until one day, as I was crossing the street to my dorm, his car whizzed around the corner and came within inches of hitting me.

Jim was clearly trying to put me in that wheelchair to live out his twisted fantasy. My biggest concern was safety. I sought protection, and met a guy, Allen, who lived in the same dorm building and was a Jiu-Jitsu martial arts competitor. I agreed to hold his sparring bags while he trained, and, in return, he agreed to accompany me when I went for runs and to class if it was dark. He also began teaching me self-defense. This tough guy was smart, funny, and handsome, and he would draw me the coolest little cartoons. I felt protected and cared for. His family was wonderful and accepted me with all of my goofy quirks.

We got engaged quickly, because he was a logical choice. He was also from Kentucky, was musically talented, and was from a Christian family. Most importantly, guys feared him because of his martial arts expertise. He was a quiet, nonintimidating guy on the surface who could remove someone's limbs with surgical precision by the time you could count to 20. The Should Monster said that was what I needed in my life at the time, to find a nice guy who checked all the boxes to marry and, as a bonus, could be scary if need be.

It just all felt void of that magical "sweep you off your feet" romance. Where were the whimsical feelings everyone described? What was it like to date others? How would I know he was the right one for me? What did being in love feel like? Was it like in the movies with couples walking around in a dreamy-headed state with goofy smiles and birds chirping all around? I asked those in happy marriages and they always responded with that same annoying answer, "You'll just know."

Well, I didn't know. I felt grateful, respected, and responsible, but not certain, unconditionally loved, or like I had met the man with whom I wanted to grow old. After a year or so, I broke things off in my junior year. I was still young and would be heading to law school in Chicago after graduation anyway. It was an amicable split, Allen remained my closest friend, and I still saw him romantically on occasion. I tried going out a few times with others to resolve this fear of never really having the chance to date, but it was too soon.

Time passed after we broke up, and I got sick. I couldn't eat anything without throwing up. The illness and dizziness continued for over a week, so I saw the school nurse. I was pregnant. I told Allen. We pulled the engagement ring out of his nightstand drawer and I methodically put it back on, neither of us feeling like we had any other choice. We devised a strategy to notify our parents. With good intentions and acting swiftly, our families went into action planning a wedding. Expectations about marriage and child-rearing rest heavy upon women across many cultures and often come with sincere intent from our friends and families because it's what they've always known.

I decided to finish my business degree locally, and forego law school in Chicago, since securing a dependable job became the top priority. It was a series of logical decisions based on social norms, financial norms, emotional norms; alternate possibilities about marriage were not considered because the Should Monster convinced me that anything veering outside the appearance of normal, acceptable, tidy, or perfect would further embarrass my family or not be supportive or healthy for the baby. It said, "It's not about you; it's about what you *should* do."

My mind returned to the present, now atop the cliff in Costa Rica. Drenched with sweat, I had climbed many miles to reach this point as my mind tumbled through lessons learned from the past. I came to the conclusion that people innocently confuse spirituality with religion, which restricts the limitless enormity of the Spirit's unconditional love into a series of man-made rules and practices. Religion is a ritual-based road map that provides the structure to guide lives into power and provide a sense of extended family, at best. At worst, it can be used to enact judgment and enforce restrictions on the decisions that we deem a threat to our way of thinking. In many cases, it represses women. What if I had actually believed that I should be physically maimed and bear children for Jim? How many women willingly enter life sentences because they think they're receiving a message from God while they're actually tuning in to the Should Monster?

The book *Sapiens* evoked an eye-opening perspective about our societies' reliance on shared myths. It was given to me in 2015 by a fellow assembly member at the Milken Institute after we worked together at a Financial Innovations Lab on Financing Green Building. The Lab was a joint venture between the Ministry of Environmental Protection and the Jerusalem Institute for Israel Studies and focused on identifying the barriers and possible solutions to developing low-carbon communities. With desert terrain, limited natural resources, and a racing demand for new housing, Israel was serious about building self-sustaining communities that recycled waste and water and were powered by renewable energy.

The event was the first think tank I'd participated in where at all times at least half of the room had on headsets that translated the conversation from a panel of interpreters who sat behind a wall in the back of the room. It was fascinating that we could carry on a conversation, each in his or her native tongue, and the signals were conveniently decoded in our ears. Visiting the wailing wall, the site of Christ's crucifixion, and his tomb was surreal. The energy felt there was like being on a spiritually induced high.

I had endless questions for the archaeologist and the locals in our group, among them were Jews, Christians, and Muslims, collaborating together with a shared goal of building more sustainable communities. I wanted to understand more about the primary local traditions, religions, modernity, and women's rights. I reckoned this endless curiosity prompted the *Sapiens* book gift. It was left with a handwritten note at my hotel on the morning of my departure back to the U.S.

Thank you for sharing your experience with us this week. We have en-joyed your contributions immensely. Our cultural divides only exist in the mind, as mankind reinvents his customs and religions to suit his current needs. I believe you will enjoy this book.

Warm regards, W.B.

I began reading the book on the taxi ride to the airport in Tel Aviv and completed it overnight as I made the journey back home. I couldn't stop reading it. All the pressures of societal "shoulds" had been made up! They weren't even real!

The book, by Yuval Noah Harari, talks about how human history was shaped by three major revolutions: the Cognitive Revolution (70,000 years ago), the Agricultural Revolution (10,000 years ago), and the Scientific Revolution (500 years ago). These revolutions emboldened people to unite around ideas that do not physically exist (such as: religion, capitalism, and politics). Harari calls the shared concepts "myths" because they are invented and agreed upon to connect groups of people based on what's happening socially at that point in time. This ability gave humans a distinct strategic advantage to dominate the animal kingdom. The myths designed are often accepted as facts to create structure, order, and camaraderie.

Page after page of *Sapiens* gave scientific and historical evidence that lifted a heavy veil, revealing that many of us blindly follow tradition in lieu of investigation. These traditions, like religions, economic structures, and politics, are, in fact, all designed to serve the needs at hand during any given point in history. The key epiphany for me was that there are many forms of traditions that have been developed over the millennia based on varying social needs but inspired by the same universal, omnipresent source of energy, or God.

While that may have been obvious to others, it was profound to me. *I had allowed my entire life to be shaped by what the* Sapiens *author termed as shared myths. Worries about what people would think, fears about pleasing them, an obsession about doing what it took to make it into Heaven … All this time, I've been free but didn't know it.* I felt relieved, misinformed, liberated, and angry all at the same time. It was a lot to process.

The more I learned about the history of mankind from that book and others, the more I realized that the religious rules we created served our social needs first then our economic wants second. Those stipulations were—and still are—sometimes used to divide us, not bring us together, with rules often cited as an excuse for exclusion rather than inclusion. But divisiveness is not what most religious founders intended.

At their core, most religious beliefs portray an inspired representation of how to interact with and exchange the boundless energy of the universe. I thought about how society had lost sight of that purpose, to love others, including our enemies, as we do ourselves and the people most like us. I wondered what common beliefs could unite us and how we could leverage that shared energy to foster connection, as if to piece together a comforting quilt crafted from the boldest colors of our true diversity—and not only our physical diversity, but also our incredible strengths, talents, and personalities that we each bring to the table.

As the mighty ocean at the base of the cliff rhythmically splashed white foamy bursts against the rocks beneath, I lost track of time on the summit far above, swimming in the realization of how much my perspective had changed since reading *Sapiens*. While there were many strong benefits of the church—like family time, social support, lifelong friendships, and shared celebrations of faith—I realized I had allowed the negative "shoulds" of religion to outweigh the joyous freedom of spirituality. We can have both structured fellowship and spiritual freedom; they're not mutually exclusive. But our eyes must be open to the most important universal truth, that unconditional love is the ultimate renewable energy resource, while hate insulates our spirit from shining its unique light into the world.

It occurred to me that this unconditional love should flow equally, without bias, among everyone. Although viewed as outdated thinking in much of Americana, the female attributes that were most greatly valued as I grew up were: submissiveness, cooperation, childbearing, fitting in, supporting others, and pleasing (at all costs). Consider, on the other hand, the highly valued attributes messaged to men from boyhood: power, strength, leadership, individuality, sexual virility, character, commanding respect, and making lots of money. *Why is it we still allow ourselves to accommodate the "shoulds" of gender bias? Why do we feel the need to fit everyone into a cookie-cutter category? Why are women called divas (or worse) for commanding respect while men are looked up to for doing the very same? Why are women shamed for sex while men are applauded for it?*

It wasn't my fault I got attacked. I didn't deserve to be stalked and put into harm's way because someone felt divinely inspired to maim me. I never had to get married—I chose to. I didn't have to hide the personal traumas going on at home. A spark had been lit within me, a welling up of passion to help other girls, moms, leaders, and people in general realize that they always have a choice. The ebb of the afternoon tide took with it the need to follow anyone's path but my own. *From this moment on, standing out is more important than fitting in.* I thought of how women are silently strong. They are great listeners. Women can multitask and communicate effectively. There's a reason why Elizabeth Warren's "Pinky Promise" went viral in an instant. Women can enjoy the infinite energy of divine love *and also* become powerful executives; we can be strength-giving moms, sisters, and wives; we can defiantly stare down the Should Monster and buck its worldly paradigms; and we can also run for President, *because that's what girls do.*

I felt deep in my bones this powerful wave of love and acceptance for myself replacing the paralysis of confinement and accommodation felt in the past. I wanted to bring along everyone who was ready to be free for themselves. Vibrantly aware that all the pent-up frustration had finally reached its tipping point and without forethought, I reached to the ground, picked up a rock about the size of a baseball and threw it with all of my might far out into the crashing waves below.

What had been holding me back from making these ripples a long time ago? It was a nagging sense that I feared failure, but of what? It was time to reframe my meaning of failure. *Failing is a part of learning and creating futures with the capacity to diverge from our pasts,* I told myself. *Embracing those failures is far more valuable than running from them or hiding them. It's worth the risk!*

A world of time and space away from my past paradigms, my mind raced with excitement at the thought of inviting a friend down to explore. While I could navigate safely within a few inland villages, driving very far along the dangerous coastline roads or into the mountains was too risky to undertake alone. I resolved that I would reserve a few more weeks of time for myself, but that it would be great to have company after that.

I considered my options with clear eyes and a brave heart: Stephen was 6'2" and incredibly handsome. He was a cross between a fitness and style magazine model with shoulder-length, unruly dark hair and a neatly trimmed, distinguished salt-and-pepper beard. His sinewy biceps were the size of my thighs and he loved hiking, Jesus, and good food. We had enjoyed six fun months of dating at arms-length after meeting randomly in a local restaurant. My intuition said Stephen represented adventure, excitement, and freedom, and I lit up just thinking about the possibilities. Each time we communicated, he expressed support and respect for my time alone. My logical Should Monster reminded me that, on the downside, we couldn't discuss politics amicably—ever. And that we hadn't spent much extended time together, so it could be risky to trust this guy.

Another option was Mike, whom I'd known for years and traveled with at times to enjoy shared interests—with my own room, of course. My logical thought was that he was a safe bet. He appeared kindhearted, loved nature and animals, and enjoyed long talks about psychology. And our political conversations were great, because we shared similar views. My intuition, however, was hesitant. Each time we talked, Mike asked me when I thought I'd be ready to jump back into a serious relationship, stressing it wasn't normal to want to be alone. He pressured to meet my friends and family and pushed to get closer. Why was he always trying to fix me? What was the big rush? Was I really broken or just comfortably independent? He also warned me about giving Stephen a chance, saying he wasn't right for me. How did he know?

All of a sudden, the habitual feedback loop of the Should Monster's voice began playing in my head: *Inviting a friend you've known for years to stay with you in Costa Rica is the logical and appropriate choice. If you scandalously invite a new romantic interest to stay with you overseas, what will people think? It could embarrass your family, and people may think you're unwise. Plus, you like him a lot. You'll have to open your heart to him, and he'll see that you haven't known how to love ever since you became damaged goods ... he'll try to get inside your heart.*

I snapped back at the realization that I was choosing to mindlessly tune in to this voice. I was allowing the drama of emotional purgatory to play out without recognizing this was a trap I was inventing for myself. I tuned out of the small-minded Should Monster AM station, imagining it grow staticky as I tuned in to a more complex frequency ... on a higher plane ... I imagined light and warmth, a Spirit force that loved me, was brave, and would guide me along the right path. There was my kick-ass Inner Owl, majestic and still. One of my favorite quotes from the Dalai Lama came to mind: "Great love and great achievements involve great risks."

Now sitting straddled atop a sturdy, fallen tree limb that protruded about two feet over the edge of the bluff, I thought of how nearly every romantic relationship I'd had with men had been directed by the Should Monster. I wondered, *If I follow my intuition, will I really feel that dreamy-headed, heart-melting love, the stuff you see in movies?* I asked myself, *What's the worst thing that happens if I invite someone to get close to me?* At that moment, I decided to *take the risk.*

I carefully dismounted the limb and began to descend back down the tree-lined cliff when a sudden revelation about the cardinals sent by Grandma Alma back home stopped me in my tracks. I hadn't thought about them since arriving in Costa Rica. Out of the blue, a crystal-clear vision popped into my head of an old state-bird quilt Grandma painted and stitched together when I was a child. The vision was like a giant "Aha!" and goosebumps rushed over me like a frigid breeze, so I knew it was my intuition speaking. But, I had no idea what the quilt meant and why it would randomly come to mind. It had been in storage for decades, somewhere buried amidst others in a large plastic tub.

Upon accessing Wi-Fi at lunch, I texted the neighborhood girls watching my cat. *Scavenger hunt! Find a light-blue-and-white quilt with state birds painted on all the white squares. Look in upstairs closets and basement. Check in the giant plastic tubs. Take photo when you find!*

Luckily, the sweet girls were on spring break that week and before my lunch was over, a photo of the quilt Grandma had hand-painted and stitched together was staring at me from my iPhone. The cardinal appeared as the state bird painted on the squares for: Illinois, Indiana, Kentucky, North Carolina, Ohio, Virginia, and West Virginia. Stephen's life had been lived mostly in Ohio and Illinois, and he had spent significant time in the other states. Mike had no known ties to any of the seven states.

A coincidence? Perhaps, but the revelation clarified for me that I had again been "should-ing" on myself by worrying about what would please everyone else instead of what *felt right to me*. I was a single executive woman in paradise and wanted a handsome, adventurous play friend. Screw it. I was ready to allow someone to get close to me without all the barricades in place. And if it made people uncomfortable that I was having too much fun, then I would thank them for their concern and then filter out their opinion as unhelpful because it didn't align with my values and wants. I gave myself permission to follow my own instinct instead of listening to a largely invented fear.

I used the FaceTime app to call Stephen and invite him to join me in exploring the waterfalls in the north, the volcanos in the east, and the beaches to the south. If allowing him into my world caused a broken heart and miffed a few protective people, so be it. I could live with that. He eagerly agreed to fly down after a few weeks. Unknowingly, facing the fear of opening my heart in that moment began the transition from being successful for the world to being fulfilled for myself. It was also the first time in my life that I hadn't felt driven to be with someone because they were "the right thing for me to do." I was allowing myself to enjoy companionship without listening to all the "shoulds" that no longer served me.

In hindsight, that day was a pivotal point in tapping into my personal power. I trusted my own intuition about what felt important in that moment and invited exactly who I wanted for a visit—taking the consequences head on for the first time since childhood. Instead of insulating myself or walling off my heart, I was finally believing in my own worthiness with an open heart. And it wasn't just *the thought* of opening my heart; I was putting action behind it, and it was incredibly energizing and empowering.

This was a feeling of *real control* unlike anything I'd felt when I was trying to control the false pretenses of the Should Monster. There was a fire in my belly, and a newfound energy had been ignited. I was grateful to have discovered this source of power, to have tapped into the guidance of my Inner Owl. I was facing a fear that had been growing for decades of allowing someone the chance to get close. Maybe he would even love me simply because—because he wanted to, not because he felt pressured into it, not because he needed me to fill something that was missing in himself, and not because tradition mandated it.

Not realizing it until heading back home a month later, not a single scorpion came into the condo after that day of revelation. I was on the path of enlightened discovery and thanked my Inner Owl for helping me recognize and win this significant battle in my ongoing war with the Should Monster.

Butterfly Effect

CHAPTER 15

Can You Hear Me Now?

Wavelength: [wave·length] n. a person's way of thinking,
especially as it affects their ability to communicate with others

Never had my dreams been so vivid and consistent as they had been since arriving in Guiones. I was not sure whether it was removing worldly distractions or some mystical portal I was tuning in to, but what I did realize was that it felt different. The cell phone Wayne and I bought in Nicoya still had no reception inside the condo. Reflecting back, it was beneficial because I had *no option* to connect to the outside world when at "home"—no radio, no TV, no phone—it was just the critters and me, yet my connectivity through dreams and intuition provided a stream of hair-raising revelations, inspiring insights, and mind-blowing new information.

One series of dreams included a young woman who used to work with me. I hadn't corresponded with her for nearly a year before the dreams, so I hadn't been consciously thinking about her. The dream journal entries reflected seemingly random insights …

Dream Journal, 23 March 2017: *I'm in a large mall with Holly. We look at tiny clothing and random items as if we're preparing for something. There is a great feeling of anticipation in the dream and then of frustration because as we visit each store, there's nobody at the cash register, so we are unable to check out. It's a sense we want to get something but cannot complete the sale. We gave up shopping and went to an elementary school where Holly wore a purple dress. She indicated she liked red or blue better, but could learn to like purple, too.*

1 April 2017: I'm walking along beside Holly while she is frenetically preparing for a very special event. She cannot find the celebration and is getting frustrated. She is clearly anticipating a major event but can't find it to get started.

I felt a gentle yet intentional urge from my Inner Owl to email Holly about the dreams because the feeling was so disappointing in them that I wanted to encourage her. I shared a highlight from the dreams with her and typed at the end:

Just letting you know that you are a powerful, strong, smart, and beautiful lady, and I'm one of your biggest advocates! Whatever you're anticipating, it will happen when it's supposed to. I'm nearly 2,000 miles away but in 'spirit,' I am supporting you and will continue to do so. :)

Holly responded to my email on the 3rd of April, 2017.

Your dreams are funny! I always find those types of dreams to be very symbolic, but even stranger that you're having the dream FOR me! Dave and I have been trying to get pregnant for 4+ months but nothing yet. It's kind of exhausting—ovulation tests, basal body temperature reading, putting all the data in a fertility app. It sounds like your dream is a prolific view into my personal struggle to get pregnant ... Hope your time down there is going well. Miss you!

Dream Journal, 16 April 2017: *Last night, I dreamt that Holly and I sat in church together behind her grandmother. It was not the grandmother I met at her wedding, but a taller lady who was thin and wore a fashionable bright orange shirt with white pants. Holly told me she was pregnant, that it was a girl, and what they were going to name her. I can't remember the name, but Lisa comes to mind. I also saw a blonde little toddler girl with big blue eyes as I awoke.*

Holly became the proud mom of a baby girl at the end of December 2017, but the baby had dark hair like her daddy. Although Holly had never met one of her grandmothers, she knew that she was tall and "really into fashion." Fast forward to 2019—the baby shed the dark hair she had at birth. Now a toddler, it had grown back in blonde. It was a nice complement to her bright blue eyes.

I've learned a lot about being patient with intuition. Naturally impatient, I wanted all the answers within my timing and neatly aligned, but it doesn't work that way. It may take years before your dreams, premonitions, and aspirations manifest.

I viewed the series of dreams as being tuned in to a wavelength, a unique frequency. Being connected occurs naturally; while, being disconnected happens as we grow up and conform. I believe we use the word "spirit" to describe natural frequencies to which we become attuned. Just like our TVs bring us pictures and sounds that are converted from waves, we are designed to be both transmitters and receivers of energy. The messages are there, we just need to leverage our energetic abilities to get in sync and find the same wavelength. It's just that, with modern distractions and skepticism about spirituality, truly tuning in to your intuition, a higher frequency, and receiving have become much more difficult.

This particular day, however, I awoke highly tuned in to my mobile phone—I had to figure out how to make it work. Determined to fix my phone problems, I snuck into the neighbor's backyard to connect to his Wi-Fi. Today, I resolved, would not pass without obtaining a cellular signal and a working phone. On my way to climb the little stone fence, I noticed my running shoes had been stolen. I had been warned never to leave shoes or personal belongings unattended in the car or on the beach but thought leaving them just outside my door to dry would be safe. *Note to self: Don't leave anything unattended.* I e-chatted online with the UAE, US, and Latin American Samsung customer service offices to no avail. I should have paid more attention to brushing up my Spanish on that app.

I drove to Nosara to the utilities provider, the Costa Rican Electricity Institute, to secure a SIM card for the new phone and procure service from the appropriate cell phone carrier for that area. Hopefully, that would solve the problem. I made a wrong turn again (most roads there were not named) and ended up on a mountaintop among million-dollar mansions. Clearly, the security station had radioed the neighborhood watch brigade, so I was promptly greeted by a group of wealthy older ladies who kindly described how to navigate my weatherworn sedan *out* of their highfalutin neighborhood and towards the utilities provider's office. I avoided an overtly snarky retort and thanked them (ahem, coughing: "Golden Girls of Guiones") for being *so* concerned about my safety that they *all* came out to help me.

Upon finally arriving at the Costa Rican Electricity Institute, the security guard said I needed to return in an hour when siesta was over, so I drove back to a local pizzeria I had passed along the way. Luckily, I had packed my laptop, so it gave me the opportunity to answer a few emails and enjoy an entire large pizza to myself (one size only) while waiting for the siesta to end. Much to the surprise and amusement of the hombres at the next table over, I had no trouble inhaling the entire thing. There were rarely sugars in the local food like there was in the U.S., so my body was feeling withdrawals from greasy, gooey, and sweetened meals. It felt like a ravenous binge every time I ate for the first couple of weeks, because my body felt this insatiable hunger.

One of the emails was from Rob. His daughters had recently arrived for a visit, so he invited me to join the family ziplining and riding horses. Thrilled at the invitation, I agreed to meet them in a couple of days at the ziplining meet-up location, 8 a.m. sharp. With an excited pep in my step, I returned to the cellular provider offices and got a new SIM card, then prepaid for service. The man wrote down the number to call and set up my voicemail, so off I went.

When I arrived back at the condo, I still got the "no service" signal. And, to make things even more exciting, when I turned the phone off and back on to reset, it requested a password for "SIM card 2." *Oh, dear.* I tried 1234. Nope. "You have two more attempts before your device will permanently lock." I tried my new phone number 8724-4249. Nope. "You have one more attempt before your device will permanently lock." Laughing to myself, *Seriously?!* I would go back to the Electricity Institute tomorrow to try and figure out how to unlock my new SIM card. I channeled my inner Kay and reconciled that communication wasn't meant to be yet.

The next morning, I traveled to the utility's office again. This time, I remembered the way without visiting the Golden Girls or using a map. Before reaching the utilities office, the dirt road was completely dug up. Men were replacing a water pipe in the middle of the roadway. Thankful to have on my remaining pair of close-toed shoes, I grabbed my backpack of belongings, and hiked the last mile or so using ditches and alleyways. People there just don't go to work if the road is under construction— things are much more laid back.

Upon arriving and dabbing off my face that was dripping with sweat, the man who had helped me the day before smiled and gave me a passcode to try. It worked. I happily walked back to the car and drove to the beach. At the beach, I ran about 5 miles, to Playa Garza and back. Much of the running over the last week I had begun doing with my eyes closed. It was my own little experiment to awaken my senses and feel the sounds, textures, and messages beyond what could be seen. It also kept my legs looking like I'd been sliding into home base without proper baseball attire.

This was my first-ever run without shoes and the last one of that distance. Feet raw with blisters and abrasions, it would take a while to toughen them up to the rocky sand. On the way back, I grabbed a Wi-Fi signal and left a Facebook post in the trusted HRC running group back home to see if anyone had advice for running barefoot on the coarse beach sand. Their advice had gotten me through many races, so surely somebody would have a good suggestion.

Once back at the little condo, the cell phone still didn't work inside, but I was able to take calls just outside the front door. Success! Content with the progress the day had brought, I pulled out the $1 watercolor paint set, purchased from the dollar store before leaving Nashville, to paint a blue butterfly I had seen that day. It wasn't exactly a Rembrandt, because I had never taken an art class and had only tried watercolors once with the neighborhood ladies, but the intent was to paint the birds and butterflies seen during my Costa Rican adventure and give them away as thank-you cards upon returning home. It's the thought that counts, right? Painting was something I never took time to learn at home, and now I had the time to try it. Despite the phone issues, the disconnections to the outer world, I was becoming increasingly connected to myself.

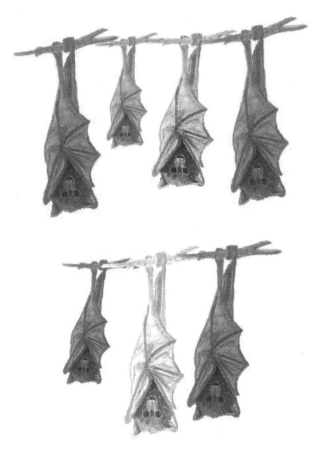

The Seven Dwarfs

CHAPTER 16

Transposition

Bat: Celtic symbolism associates bats with being a spiritual navigator. Because the bat hangs upside-down, Celts gave this night creature the symbolic value of transposition—akin to being reborn.

As the days passed, I found myself establishing routines. For example, I spent about an hour doing a blend of improvised yoga that was plucked randomly from the practices of Bikram, Vinyasa, and YMCA methods. In the extreme heat of Guiones, it was easy to work up the same sweat as if I was still alongside Kay in the hot-yoga studio back home. As the hour passed, my body grew exhausted, but my intuition ignited.

There was a thatch-covered area about 12 feet by 10 feet outside the little condo I rented. The area was a couple stories above ground level in front of a huge, gorgeous tree with sprawling branches in every direction. I laid a towel on the concrete and always did the poses facing the giant tree. After the third day, local participants joined. Even though it was morning or midday when I exercised (to avoid the intense afternoon heat), cute little brown bats lit underneath the thatch and hung out with me while I sweated, inverted, and sorted out the meaning of life.

Although I grew up on a farm, I hadn't been this close to bats before. Their little conversational chirps sounded like a bird with a sinus infection, stuffy little clicks and squeaks. At first, there were just a couple, but after over a week's time, there were seven. I named them after the adorable characters in the old Disney film *Snow White and the Seven Dwarfs*: Dopey, Doc, Bashful, Happy, Grumpy, Sleepy, and Sneezy. Truth be told, I had trouble telling the quiet ones, Bashful, Sleepy, and Doc, apart during their daily visits.

In 2006, when working on a partnership with the San Diego Zoo to raise awareness about endangered species, they suggested we create a positive brand around bats. We used misunderstood animals as our mascots for the SYNERGY conservation program that helped over 40,000 military families reduce energy and water consumption. From that program, I recalled learning that, contrary to a common myth, bats are not blind and could see just fine, in the daytime and at night. They use echolocation, or the high-frequency sonar sounds that bounce off objects, to obtain extra-sensory information that accentuates what they see with their eyes. It adds a layer of accuracy and speed as they navigate in the dark.

Bats can't take off from the ground; that's why they hang upside-down. They have to literally let go in order to soar. Otherwise, they'll never reach the heights where they were designed to fly, where their nourishment lives, and where they could escape the threat of predators. They are also very sensitive, as they constantly gather the signs around them. It was the same type of wayfinding I was learning. My world was upside-down and I was in the process of learning to let go in order to feel the freedom of flight and to find the nourishment that could feed the rediscovery of my true power. Guiones had become my cave, the safe place to seek refuge from harm and regenerate, and I was learning to tune in to senses beyond what we usually deploy in order to finally confront the darkness.

After yoga, I met Rob and his daughters for ziplining. The girls were delightful, fun, and wise beyond their years. We piled into the back of a large, old 2-ton truck with a dozen other tourists who had driven to the area from across Costa Rica to take flight high above the jungle canopy on one of the longest ziplines in the world. With 21 runs totaling over 11 kilometers (6.8 miles) in length, the longest single line was over 750 meters (approximately half a mile). The truck had no safety rails or seat belts. Everyone sat around the perimeter or on a bench nailed to the truck bed in the middle. We were on pothole-laden paved roads and dirt roads for about 20 miles. The manual gears on the old truck made a grinding sound as the vehicle hauled the passengers up the seriously steep, winding hills of the jungle. Twice, the vehicle stuttered and jolted back and forth as it nearly choked out while making its way up the terrain. The last half of the journey was on one-lane roads with no safety rails alongside the steep curves. I told myself the zipline itself would be a breeze compared to the gripping ride up to the mountaintops.

We arrived safely, shared a few fist bumps in relief, and each took a moment to collect ourselves as we were helped out of the giant truck bed onto the patch of dirt at the road's end. After gearing up, rehydrating, and learning the safety instructions, each person began the descent. My confidence grew quickly with each plunge. Because these lines lasted up to an unbelievable half-mile in length, it allowed enough time to let go of the worries of safely stopping long enough to enjoy the flight.

High above the canopy, I became a bird at home in the sky with the wind on my face and an untamable spirit of joy swelling in my chest. I chose not to be a bat, because I don't like eating mosquitoes. Instead, I chose to be a hawk, because they soar high above the trees and have keen vision and power. By the time we were halfway through, I'd learned how to flip upside-down. It felt like doing flips across Grandma's lawn again—right-side up and upside-down, perspectives changing as my life was literally becoming transposed.

On the way back from the ziplining adventure, I stopped by the post office in Nosara. It was about the size of a standard home's living room, so I accidentally passed it twice before finding it. The post office was the closest destination a package could be mailed to me while staying at the rural condo, and I received notification from Randy that my box of ant traps, sunscreen, eye drops, and spaghetti sauce should be waiting. I think if I would have asked him to wrestle an alligator, he would have also obliged. He's the kind of guy everybody wants on their team. He makes things happen and authentically cares for others.

After attempting my best Spanish to retrieve the box from amidst a pile on the back wall of the tiny room, the anticipated package was placed in my hands. It felt like Christmas morning, except the box was held together with duct tape, barely hanging on structurally with damp sides. What in the world was in there? The smell was putrid, and I drove with windows down in the car the rest of the way home, despite being pummeled with dust from the roads. Finally able to cut it open upon arrival, I realized Randy had generously sent two bottles of spaghetti sauce, each of which had exploded during the trip. In the extreme heat, the sauce had taken on a life of its own, literally overtaking everything else in the package as its giant, living petri dish.

Everything was covered in red sauce and green mold. The box's sides peeled back easily as they were soaked in the Christmas-colored mixture. The smell was so strong I had to conduct this surgical procedure outside in the open air. I gently sorted the broken glass and carefully extracted the new valuables, rinsing each to remove any remaining bits of sauce and mold. The sunscreen, ChapStick, eye drops, mosquito repellant, and ant traps had been rescued. It was one of the most appreciated gifts and was much needed at the time. It felt good to have someone from back home concerned about me.

The entire day had been a gift. Freedom was emerging like I hadn't felt in decades. And it was becoming more frequent. The more I recognized and leaned into those feelings, letting go of what people may think or how silly I surely looked, the more often my instincts returned. Energetically, I was learning how to recharge that inner spark that burned out long ago. The connectedness of the universe was coming into focus, but not through the use of my eyes, it was becoming clear through my heart. A trend was emerging. I was getting closer to solving this internal puzzle—*the most powerful gifts of insight came when I was allowing, observing, and listening instead of thinking, solving, and controlling.*

It would be difficult to top this day. By the time I got back to the condo that evening, I sliced up a mango found along the roadway to accompany an entire box of Cheerios. Clearly, my cooking style was more about efficiency than extravagance. My ant friends welcomed me home. I was so excited from the events of the day that being without power and having a cold shower didn't faze me. I cleaned up, set my old-school alarm clock, and did the ritual dressing for bedtime. The ritual was aimed at scorpion-crawl-up-your-pants prevention while I slept. It hadn't happened yet, but after finding one under my covers and another inside the pillowcase, I imagined them still making their plans under the bed for a nighttime attack. *Pants tucked securely into socks? Check! Shirt tucked firmly into pants? Check! See you in the morning, ants.*

Samson

CHAPTER 17

The Floodgates Have Opened

Howler Monkey: The howler monkey is the eleventh-day sign of the ancient Mayan zodiac. It symbolizes joining the past, present, and future. According to legend, the monkey gives us a connection to our subconscious awareness through common ground that we all share.

A scorpion-free night—it felt like I had won the lottery. It had been many days since seeing the last clawed critter, but I was still painfully paranoid, looking under everything before stepping, sitting, or lying near it, but each day the fear subsided a bit.

There was a gnawing part of me still viscerally connected to my professional accomplishments, so naturally the Should Monster attacked an area where I shined. My career was both my personal identity and my steadfast, dependable companion. My spirit was restless. Emails flooded in from friends and former colleagues, "What do you have planned?" "What are you going to do next?" "Are you sure a trip is what you need right now instead of a secure job?" I reminded myself that I was frustrated but *free*, and for the first time in my adult life, I wasn't concerned about meeting the next deadline.

There was an energy inside that I had begun tapping into more frequently. It had been aching to be heard, but I was still figuring out how to listen. For millennia, philosophers, prophets, and religious leaders have been able to tap into the spiritual realm. How hard could it be, after all? Like everything else, one logically should be able to learn about it, set a goal, then accomplish it. Incapable of sitting still for more than a few minutes at a time, I was daunted by the thought of traditional meditation. I read books, tried different types of yoga and Tai Chi, but to little avail. There were few ways to quiet this mind without becoming physically exhausted first. There had to be a better way. It was proving difficult for me, but deep in this rural place I was finding new ways of tuning in to the spirit within. Tuning in, it occurred to me, was different for every human. We all are unique and therefore each person's method of "hearing" their own distinct spirit animal—or inner voice, image, feeling, or any number of things—would be just as unique.

The day was spent writing, acknowledging, and reading, with focus on letting go of my failed marriages. Not surprisingly, Allen and I never made a real go of it. On paper, the first marriage may have lasted a year or so. In reality, I don't think either of us acknowledge it as a strong effort since we lived in different places and had tied the knot under what felt like insurmountable pressures during college. I was used to, and comfortable with, managing by myself with Trent, but eventually moved from Louisville back to my hometown to save on childcare expenses. My mother had just retired from teaching and offered to help with the baby. Having my parents involved was an absolute gift at that point in my life. Allen and his family maintained warm relations with both Trent and me that continue to this day.

I was single a short time before Charlie asked me out. We had been friends before college, and he and his family were very kind to Trent and me. Being a single mom in a small town was like having a scarlet letter painted across your chest. Churchgoers in every chapel, the people at work, everyone, it seemed, wanted to know, "Where's his daddy?" or "Where's your husband?" The local, well-intentioned culture was obsessed with my being unmarried with a baby, and along with those "shoulds," I allowed myself to feel like a second-class citizen in those settings.

On the contrary, I was doing just fine with it everywhere else. Trent and I didn't have much money, but we'd share oatmeal at breakfast and a box of rice for supper. He contently slept in the grocery cart once a week at 4 a.m., as before work was the only time I had to grocery-shop. My after-work routine was filled with classes, coursework, dinner, and story time. He was the most perfect and wonderful thing about my life, and I was abundantly grateful for him. I turned Charlie down a few times, uncertain he fully understood what he was getting himself into, before he convinced me to go to dinner. We bought diapers on the way home. He surprised me with hand-picked flowers on occasion, sweet little notes, and took Trent to play with the animals on his family's farm.

Within a few months, Charlie began to ask about marriage. He was excited about the possibility of spending Christmas morning with Trent—which, of course, would be impossible if we weren't married first. Charlie had loving intentions, and the Should Monster reinforced his case by whispering that I would be depriving Trent of a father figure if I didn't get married right away, since his biological dad lived elsewhere. Besides, people would stop judging me and focus on my friendship or my work ethic instead of my love life.

At that point, I didn't feel much, especially romantically, given my experience with men. The barrier was securely built around my heart. The series of events left me feeling—no, thinking—I just needed to execute whatever needed to be done. *Suck it up! Soldier on! Be the best employee, student, mom, and girlfriend-fiancé-wife that you can be. And hurry up about it!* Charlie was nice to me, and I felt that I should, so, without a thought of hesitation: "Yes. I do. Again."

A few years into the marriage, we realized we had dramatically different interests and life goals, like where we wanted to live, appropriate jobs for moms, how to raise children, whether to attend church—you know, just the basic foundations of every strong marriage. As mentioned, the flowers and notes, and even the birthday cards, ceased. Charlie's father passed, triggering even more unresolved unhappiness. We coexisted as best we could for the next 18 years. Needless to say, I was shocked to receive 22 pages of handwritten letters from Charlie a couple years after the divorce.

He penned the letters on the previous Mother's Day and Thanksgiving, but they arrived in my mailbox mid-December, just after I resigned from my job and before preparing to journey to Costa Rica.

I glanced at the letters when they were received, but taped the envelope shut and stuck it in the closet, not ready to process the words neatly scribed on the pages. Charlie was well educated, wrote articulately, and always found my dangling participles. I grabbed the envelope on the way out the door to Guiones and now found myself retrieving it shakily from the zipper pocket of my red suitcase, as if it could sting me like a scorpion. I realized there was no postmark on it, so it was hand-delivered from a city hours away (he probably left it when working in the area). It had been a couple of years since the divorce, yet it seemed the longer we were separated, the more Charlie realized he missed me. I missed the Charlie who loved me decades earlier.

In the letters, Charlie apologized. He noticed he loved me once he was alone. Dozens of painful, repressed recollections crept onto the sofa beside me as I read page after page. The memories were real, and they cut deeply, but those events were finished and not to be endured again. I let go. I forgave him and declared any remaining feelings of regret or resentment to be released. I went to Scorpion Hill and lit fire to the letters. Watching the flames engulf the pages, one by one, I felt thick layers of burden wisp away like smoke from my soul. As I carefully placed beautifully colored leaves from a nearby plant atop the ashes, as if to leave them in peace, there was only love left in my heart for Charlie. True progress, I thought logically to myself as if in third person. I felt the pain, relief, forgiveness, and peace of love.

Japanese samurai warriors reminded themselves of the inevitability of loss with a phrase: "Die before going into battle." This allowed a warrior to envision or feel the worst possible outcome, death, before the fight began. The practice freed him from the fear of dying during the actual battle, because he had already experienced it in his mind. This method is also used to help executives today and is referenced in the book *The Last Word on Power* by Tracy Goss.

I often used a variation of the samurai technique when making important decisions that involved risk, "What's the *worst* thing that can happen?" It was typically something like upsetting someone I cared about, losing a job, or looking stupid. It also worked well with listening to my intuition—*If I follow what this illogical feeling or voice is telling me, what's the worst thing that can happen?*

I was preparing for the ultimate battle with the Should Monster—of identifying it, confronting it, and leveraging my newly strengthened Inner Owl to overcome it. Using the samurai technique, I decided it was time to "die" just prior to bedtime. They would find me in bed, overwhelmed with scorpion bites, and no longer breathing. I'd be in a gray t-shirt and navy lounge pants stuffed neatly into my purple Converse mid-calf socks. Nobody would be looking for me since I was not communicating much with the folks back home. It would likely be Luis, the property manager, who would find me when he returned to finish fixing the AC.

Luis would call Mark, the condo owner, who would call Randy, my friend who helped me locate this place, who would call Brenda, my parents' neighbor, who would tell my parents. They'll call Trent first and he would tell his younger brother, Ethan. There's no fear about my salvation—I've been both dunked (Baptist) and sprinkled (Methodist), so if there's a religious rite that gets me in the Pearly Gates, that box had been checked. Twice. My financial information was already in Trent's hands, so he'd handle sorting the insurance and oversee Ethan's college savings.

Mom would call Kay and ask her to tell my other friends. Scott, the associate pastor at my parents' church, would give a service, and my remains would be cremated then scattered over a body of water. I left the instructions vague because it really doesn't matter what they do with my lifeless body—it would be swollen from scorpion stings and my energy would long since be floating somewhere else.

Tabitha Ann Scott / Strambel / Cramer / and again Scott is dead. All of the challenges and victories are over. I logically declared it all finished without much emotion and fell quickly into my entertaining Costa Rican dreamscape.

The next morning, I grabbed plenty of water and headed to my favorite trail through the jungle. Another 100-degree day with a flood of memories seeping through the cracks of the restrictive dam wall in my mind, it felt comforting to set foot onto the familiar trail in the cooling shade of the jungle canopy. An awkward-looking coatimundi family quickly descended their trees to greet me. They looked like a mash-up of raccoons, opossums, and anteaters. The first time this happened, I thought they were going to attack—it was horrifying! Over time, I figured out they were just curious and liked to come down from the treetops to see who was visiting.

I also became accustomed to the howler monkeys in the forest canopy. The alpha male I called Samson usually gave me the traditional booming warning when I would pass through. It was mortifying the first time I heard it, but locals had warned me that the roaring that sounded like an angry lion was just coming from the male monkeys as a notice that they stood ready to defend their territory.

Stepping over the roots of my favorite tree, which was an awe-inspiring fourteen feet in diameter, I began reflecting on all the things that had been left behind when I "died" last night. I thought of what it must have been like to be Ethan—to have gone from being the traveling soccer team's star goalie to watching the action from the confines of his wheelchair or crutches. None of his friends, even the megachurch youth minister's son, one of his closest friends before the surgeries, bothered to visit.

I thought about Trent, always clear in his vision of becoming a pilot in the Air Force, and how it must have felt to hear the words "no cure" and to even lose his driver's license until his disorder could be regulated. I wondered what depth of sadness he felt when scribing the words I found crumpled on a piece of notebook paper under the sofa, *I don't want to live like this anymore. I'm lying here contemplating how to end it all but am too damn tired to get up and do it.* There was no homecoming dance or senior prom or application to be sent for military service. Was college even an option? A lifetime of dreams had been ripped from beneath him. It wasn't fair.

I thought about waking alone in a ditch at that party as a teen. Instead of thinking, *Am I ok? Do I need stitches? Were there any witnesses? Who can I go to for help?*—all I could think of was hoping nobody ever found out. The overwhelming fear of the "shoulds" and labels, the guilt for putting myself in the situation, and avoidance of the lectures that would follow far outweighed the need to take care of myself. My trust and heart were left in the ditch that night alongside the tire iron that was used to knock me out. The headaches were excruciating for months afterwards. I remember laying my head down on my desk at school and pretending to be somewhere deep underwater, swimming peacefully and weightlessly with dolphins or whales, until the pain subsided.

I remembered the frustration of being told our company would gain the use of two facilities for which we had been negotiating if I agreed to spend a weekend on the owner's yacht in the Bahamas with him. I recalled being slammed against the side of the west Pentagon elevator and forcibly kissed by a high-ranking officer as the Close Door button was suppressed. And the time I was abandoned at a restaurant in a strange city by a business colleague of equal rank after turning down his advances. In a time before Uber and mobile phones, I walked the 5 miles back to our hotel at night in a suit and dress shoes.

These were mere speed bumps along the successful career highway. I'd never let them affect me or slow me down. Even though the vast majority of male colleagues were respectful, when there was an instance of harassment, it was important to discern whether raising a red flag would create more harm than justice. It was never a simple black-and-white rule with "right" clearly opposing "wrong"; each case had a web of complex circumstances and consequences, and was dealt with in an appropriate way.

As I thought about how much I wanted to be protected from it all, my jogging increased in speed, as if I could outrun the painful feelings that kept reeling through my mind. I thought, *Who would even miss me if I never came out of this literal and figurative jungle?* Then it happened again. Tears. This was the second time I let them fully slip out in God knows how many decades. Not soft rolling tears, like the night I arrived, but ugly, gut-wrenching belly cries rang out. My running slowed to a stop. There wasn't enough oxygen to keep moving. I had to stop and ... feel. Tired. Frustrated. Angry. Alone. Fully emotionally connected.

Suddenly I heard a deep, sorrowful cry. It was very loud and stopped me cold in my tracks, a distraction from my own deluge of tears. Momentarily frightened someone was in the jungle mocking me, I ducked behind a large tree and kept listening. It was getting closer. Frozen now with fear, I couldn't move. It was coming from above, getting louder. I was silent.

It was Samson, who was now just six feet above me in the tree I was hiding behind. I didn't know monkeys could cry. I'd never heard anything so sorrowful or odd. He heard me. He stopped the others from their terrifying screeches and howling and shared a moment of sadness with this strange human. I paused in profound shock, honor, disbelief, and joy. Goosebumps covered every square inch of my body as I gazed directly at Samson and consoled him. I thanked him for loving me.

My frustrations turned to wonder and appreciation for this revelation. We were connected. The monkeys, the trees, dreams of the future, memories from the past, the birds, the snakes, and even those damn scorpions … We were all inextricably woven from the same energy to be born again and again through the ages, to grow, mature, decline, and begin again. This same energy was the source of every major religion, self-help book, business methodology—if it involved growth, it was simply another method of optimizing our own universal, renewable source of personal power. This real-time broadcast was brought to me courtesy of my Inner Owl, and I was finally tuned in enough to witness it live and unfolding before me.

Feeling was not the weakness the Should Monster warned me against; it was instead the gateway to ultimate power. It was the chasm between a lifetime of striving to embody society's definition of *success* from a future of true *fulfillment*. All the logic in the world catapulted me to executive heights, but it took allowing my heart to feel again to comprehend what was truly valuable. I didn't need protection from anything—there was more power already inside me than I could have imagined possible. *Everybody already has the ability to reconnect like this*, I thought. *But who would believe it?*

Upon returning to the condo, I climbed to the yoga spot across from the giant, sprawling tree. There were only three bats upon my arrival, but as the afternoon slipped into evening, the remaining little fellas came along to hang out. Logically, my mind struggled to comprehend how I was becoming so interconnected.

The days began to take on a rhythm. One day, I found my yoga spot's thatch roof being dismantled by the property manager. Clearly the other residents were less enamored with the Seven Dwarfs than I was. I wondered if they realized they had just shooed away seven helpers that each ate over 1,000 insects an hour. So much for this being a mosquito-free trip. (Dang it!) I headed to the beach access spot in Guiones where a large grove of trees provided enough shelter from the sun to complete my daily hour of yoga.

Since the closest place to buy new sneakers was over an hour's drive, duct tape over the soles of my feet were my new running shoes, thanks to my friend Tammy's response to my inquiry to the HRC running club back home. Tape worked like a champ protecting my feet from the grainy sands, and there was no cleanup necessary. After a few early sliding incidents, I learned to leave gaps between each piece of tape to create traction. In addition, my manual transmission skills were becoming finely tuned. I could drive a stick-shift up or down any hill without choking out the engine. Things were certainly falling into place.

I began to see why people would retire to little villages near the sea. There was peace in the pace and the obstacles that arose seemed small in comparison to the mental stress of the modern world. Back home, success was largely defined by the number and extravagance of things you could buy. The bigger house required greater debt which required more work, often leading to a vicious cycle in pursuit of stuff. But happiness simply doesn't require stuff. Happiness, I was learning, was found in truly feeling and living in connection with the natural world around us and inside us.

It was finally time to meet Rob and his daughters to ride horses on the beach. This had been a lifelong fantasy—to experience two of my favorite things, horses and the ocean, at the same time. I was grateful to have been included with their family. The Americans in this area were gracious and unpretentious. When I arrived, Rob's daughters were sipping on smoothies while waiting for the horses to be unloaded and saddled.

The guide was doing his best to communicate with us in English. He asked each rider's experience level—one of us would have to take Spirit, a beautiful buckskin-colored horse with a jet-black mane and tail. He was sweet, but temperamental. I gleefully volunteered.

My horse Betty's first foal was a filly we named Savannah. Like Spirit, her coat was a sleek buckskin tan color with a black mane and tail. Both Spirit and Savannah were adorned with a white diamond on their foreheads and a white anklet on their rear left foot. Convinced this would be my best day yet, I climbed upon Spirit's strong back and gently untucked the part of his mane that had been stretched taut under the saddle. He shifted his hind legs side to side, then pawed at the sand with his front hoof—something horses do when they want to get going.

Everyone was finally mounted up, and off we went. There was a trail just off the beach with brush and small trees, 15 feet or shorter, dwarfed in comparison to the jungle trees to which I was now accustomed. The trail wound past a tiny cemetery I had never noticed, then up onto the bluff trails I had explored the day I decided to ask Stephen to visit. The view from atop Spirit's strong back was incredible. I felt full of love and gratitude—for this horse, for the people around me, for the friends and family back home, for my health, and for this opportunity. Without a spoken word, my heart fully connected with the giant beast. Our ride lasted about an hour, but it seemed like 10 minutes. I dismounted and gave Spirit a long hug and gently smooched his whiskery nose.

Before I knew it, it was Easter Sunday. Limo Dan hosted Easter Dinner in the area where I used to do bat-yoga. The owner of a local restaurant and a few old friends of Dan's came. Everyone brought something. My job was bringing drinks. (I wondered who had tipped them off about my poor cooking skills.) Dan roasted pork and made different types of salsas for street tacos. Some were traditional tomato, onion, and spices, but my favorite were the ones with watermelon, pineapple, and mangos. I'd never had pork with fruit salsa on a taco, but it's something I've cooked many times since. We cut up fresh avocados and drank to new friends, great food, and the Easter holiday. *Pura vida!*

Only a couple more days until I would pick up Stephen at the airport. I began preparing to have someone else in the little condo by sweeping up, buying some proper groceries, and stocking up on water. Standing outside of Limo Dan's office in Guiones to borrow the Wi-Fi, I used FaceTime for one last call with Stephen to align on pickup details. I was nervously excited about his visit. It would allow me to explore the more remote and difficult areas of the country and enable me to share this beautiful place with someone else.

Gratitude

CHAPTER 18

Jump with Me

Vulnerability is the only authentic state. Being vulnerable means being open, for wounding, but also for pleasure. Being open to the wounds of life means also being open to the bounty and beauty. Don't mask or deny your vulnerability: It is your greatest asset. Be vulnerable: Quake and shake in your boots with it. The new goodness that is coming to you, in the form of people, situations, and things can only come to you when you are vulnerable.

— STEPHEN RUSSELL

Stephen was expected midday at the airport. I was nervous about seeing him after months of being apart. *Would we still have chemistry? Would he be happy here without Wi-Fi and cell service? Would he get bored and want to go home?* It took me nearly three hours to drive to Liberia's airport to pick him up. A little over halfway there, I stopped at KFC in Nicoya because, obviously, there's just something about mashed potatoes and brown gravy that settles my nerves. In my humble opinion, it's the ultimate comfort food. By this time, I proudly ordered in Spanish.

Upon arriving at the airport about the time his flight would land, I unpacked my laptop to check in on the pets back home and see if there was anything interesting I was missing. I removed my sandals and sat cross-legged on the floor because it was cooler than the sticky black plastic chairs in the hallway outside of customs. Who knew how long it would take him after landing to get through the customs process. I received an update that my dog was ill back home, so my mother had picked her up to visit the farm in Kentucky until I returned. Poor girl. The dog was 15 years old and had been shot twice. Not by me, of course, but she was a rescue dog from the pound and upon having X-rays a few years ago they noticed the bullets still inside. I was confident she would be spoiled rotten by the time I returned home.

I received a text: *Just finished customs.* I watched the double doors with anticipation and when he walked through them, my heart skipped a beat—maybe two. Stephen had a pink Tab cola T-shirt on with his long hair tied back in a sleek ponytail. He was the most beautiful man I had seen in a long time. I ran the 50 feet to greet him—so excited, I completely forgot about being barefoot. His strong arms held two suitcases and a tennis racket in one hand, and he scooped me up like a tiny doll with his other for an embrace I'll never forget. He missed me. I missed him. It felt great. There was no air conditioning in the airport and the temperature outside was the usual hot, dry 100, but the energy I felt from this embrace … this smoldering kiss … was far hotter.

As we left the airport, Stephen waved goodbye to Larry and Musica, a sweet couple in their late 60s he sat next to on the flight. Larry was giving him a thumbs up in approval of our embrace. They discussed restaurants, places of interest, and side trips during the flight. The couple was from San Antonio, Texas, and mentioned they'd be staying about an hour south of Guiones in Palado Samara.

We drove north to Rio Celeste to spend a couple of nights visiting the blue waters and the Rincon de la Vieja volcano. For our stay, Stephen had selected Tenorio Lodge, owned by a retired couple from France, Louis and Charlotte. Louis was eager to discuss my hiking goals in the area with all sorts of maps while Charlotte and Stephen exchanged dinner plans and check-in logistics in French. We had our own chalet overlooking one of the smaller volcanoes and dozens of types of birds, butterflies, frogs, and monkeys flitted, hopped, and scampered around the abode.

The first evening we visited a nearby preserve to see some of the amazing local animals up close. I had been dying to see a sloth, and this preserve had a few, so I was excited and filled with anticipation. The entrance to the preserve was a long hanging bridge, which we crossed, following our guide who spoke no English. We saw the giant tree supposedly used in the movie *Avatar*—the trees there were incredible! This was a different subclimate in the north of the country; it was damp and more like a rainforest. Our sandals slid across the slippery paths as we witnessed tiny pea-sized frogs, giant tortoises, and all sorts of exotic birds. No sloths out today, but we were thrilled with the adventures of our first day together in a long time. Two muddy, happy messes, we returned to the chalet where he rested while I painted some of the many beautiful birds we had seen. I never paid much attention to birds in the past, but for some reason on this trip I became drawn to them.

It rained that night near Liberia for about an hour and the next morning at sunrise. The moon shone so brightly through the tall glass wall overlooking the volcano that I spent hours in bed watching it cross the sky. Any doubt that I'd made the right decision to ask Stephen to visit was erased. This man made me happy in my bones. We joined other guests at the lodge for breakfast before heading out. Stephen discussed proper coffee with Charlotte, again dusting off the French he learned while living in France with his family as a teen. Meanwhile, I inhaled a few pancakes and uploaded some photos to share with friends back home.

Later we packed our things and headed out the half-mile back to the main road, but someone was blocking the driveway. It was Charlotte, she was motioning us to pull over. Concerned that something was wrong, we stopped and exited the vehicle. She hushed us, leading us over to the edge of the woods about 20 meters from the driveway. Baffled, we followed.

She pointed to the ground at the base of a narrow tree, then followed its trunk with her pointed finger, stopping midway to the top. As our eyes followed upwards, we saw him. It was a giant sloth! He was just hanging around minding his own business, so we respectfully took a few photos and gave Charlotte a warm embrace before returning to the car. Surely this was a dream and I would awaken at any minute, but before the veil of the dream was lifted, I wanted to savor it longer. I was ready for the risk of loving someone and letting him into my world. I enjoyed this man and his sweet, pure soul. He had experienced a couple years of self-reflection recently, as well, after literally going blind in one eye and nearly blind in the other. A painstaking series of eight surgeries repaired his vision, but the experience created appreciation and humility.

As an infant, Stephen had been adopted by two loving, wonderful parents. Their biological son had passed away of a hereditary heart condition at the age of five months. Although still stricken with grief months after the baby's death and raising three daughters already, his parents were approached about a baby boy needing a home. They immediately agreed and took Stephen home just days later. His Biblical name, which meant "reward," embodied their strong faith and gratitude. His parents went on to adopt another son within the next year—growing their family to five children.

Stephen temporarily stayed with his parents to recover from the final eye surgeries. He and his mother were always close, through his moves, his ups and downs, and especially through his series of grueling eye surgeries. One afternoon while his dad was at the dentist, Stephen made tea for his mom. Upon bringing the cup to share it with her, he found she was having a massive stroke. He went into action—called the ambulance, rode to the hospital, transferred her to another hospital, contacted the rest of the family, and prayed with every fiber that her life would be spared. She made a miraculous recovery and Stephen's perspective on life would be forever changed. He felt his mother's selfless act of adopting him saved his life, and she will tell you that Stephen's quick response and prayers helped save hers in return. Those changes that happened to him and the changes that were happening to me perfectly prepared us for each other in that very moment. Neither of us had been so openly vulnerable until this point in our lives.

Rio Celeste Waterfall in Tenorio National Park

CHAPTER 19

Rio Celeste

Synchronicity happens when we align with the flow of the universe rather than insisting the universe flow our way.

— AKEMI G

We drove to Rio Celeste, which means "heavenly river," and hiked the Volcano Tenorio. Legend has it the waters are so blue because God used the point where two rivers meet to dip his paintbrush after finishing the sky. It was absolutely breathtaking! Long thought to have been caused by volcanic minerals in the water, scientists recently proved that the bright turquoise waters are an optical illusion created by the light reflecting off aluminosilicates that cover rocks on the riverbed. A day of hiking and afternoon of getting reacquainted was just what we needed.

Rincon de la Vieja means "ring of the old woman." It's the tallest volcano in northern Costa Rica and is active, so unfortunately visitors are no longer permitted to visit the summit due to recent volcanic activity. We hiked a 6-mile trail through the rainforest to a 6,100-foot elevation where a waterfall fell deep into the canyon below. The trail wove through a dense jungle with multiple tribes of monkeys—we saw capuchins, a tan-colored large-monkey clan, and what looked like spider monkeys.

Giant blue butterflies were everywhere. We saw large peacock-like birds and all sorts of creatures along the way before the trail left the tree line and ascended into rocky plains in the clouds. It was a challenging hike, even for two very fit people. When we reached the summit, we drank the crystal water from the falls and took a short snack break before returning back to the national park area. Along the way, we stopped and sat atop a giant fallen tree. At 5'8", I didn't reach half the diameter of its roots. We prayed aloud with gratitude to God for the day, the experiences, and each other.

I've never been around a man who encouraged me to pray aloud. It felt odd and awkward. I didn't have trouble speaking to the Spirit when in the jungle alone, but it seemed weird to say those things out loud … nonetheless, I gave it a shot and survived. I've never dated a guy who grabs my hand at dinner and says a blessing out loud—a prayer that always included thanks for me. Stephen's presence served a valuable purpose. It taught me to be unafraid to show love and appreciation; that it was OK to risk looking foolish because the reward was an open heart with increased connectivity to myself, the Spirit, and others.

We dropped off our rental car in Liberia and caught a ride to Limo Dan's car service back in Guiones where we picked up a small 4x4 SUV. It would be much better on the roads here than the car I had driven the first month. We drove to dinner nearby and finally arrived at the condo after dark. As I instinctively reached for the key on the rental car key fob, it hit me. I had left the condo key in Liberia at the car rental company, where it was still on the keychain. Frustration. Exhaustion. Guilt. Cringing in disbelief, *how could I be so stupid?* My experience and instinct led me to expect great wrath for not remembering. I braced for the impact of yelling that would be coming my way.

I was able to reach Ed, the realtor who met me my first day in town, to get another key, but he was 90 minutes away. About that time, the neighbor in the condo adjacent to mine pulled in. We explained what happened and he invited us in. His name was Mauricio but he said people call him Mau. It all happened so fast and Stephen finally spoke. His words surprised and disarmed me. Speaking first to Mau, he mentioned that he had just traveled in from Nashville and brought some Tennessee Fireball whiskey. "Mau, would you like to give it a try?"

Then to me, "It's just 90 minutes before Ed will be here. Let's get to know your neighbor and have a drink." We shared the bottle of whiskey that Stephen brought from Tennessee as payment to Mau for his kindness. Mau was the IT guy for the four-star Harmony Hotel in town. He was from the capital city of San José and had lived here about a month. His English was so perfect, we thought he was American. Mau shared his love of music and performing—we talked him into playing his guitar and singing a couple songs after a few drinks. He dubbed Stephen as Thor for his bulging biceps, long hair, and blue eyes—he certainly stood out as an oddity in rural Costa Rica.

Once Ed arrived, he didn't miss the opportunity to taste the Tennessee whiskey. They don't often sell specialty liquors like Fireball there. What started as utter frustration ended in a fun night of singing, listening, and getting to know some really nice people. Welcome to this part of the world—*Pura vida!*

Day one for Stephen in Guiones was a shock. He couldn't believe I'd ridden my bicycle on these roads and remote places before getting a car. After running errands, we hiked a few miles to the beautiful overlook where so many epiphanies had occurred in prior months. While I thought to pack snacks and extra water, we left them in the car. I miscalculated the heat and distance. My sunscreen had long since sweated off and our water ran out. Kicking myself, we hiked to Lagarta Lodge, the other four-star hotel nestled high on the cliffs nearby, rather than trying to make it back.

Embarrassed and beginning to shake from lack of calories, I explained to the manager I needed to get some sugar in my system right away, but that we didn't have any money. His name was Adam and he graciously gave us watermelon and bananas and refilled our 24-ounce bottles twice with chilled water. I recovered within about 15 minutes, so we headed back to the car. We vowed to go back soon to have dinner and thank Adam properly for his generosity.

While walking back, we decided to take the back roads instead of the beach, as there would be some shade to block the sun's rays. A car pulled over and a voice from within said, "Hey, you're the guy from the plane!"

It was Larry and Musica. They had been searching for new beach areas to enjoy and had gotten lost. We advised them to follow the signs to Lagarta Lodge and look for Adam—that the hotel would have a map, a great meal, and directions for them. Stephen lit up and got goosebumps himself.

I laughed and said "You see what I mean about this place? Seriously, with their hotel being over an hour's drive from here, what are the odds of running into the couple from your flight?!" If one variable leading to that moment had changed—if I had remembered the snacks, if Larry and Musica hadn't been lost, if we didn't take an alternate route back from the hotel—this encounter would have never happened.

Stairs in La Fortuna National Park

CHAPTER 20

Fear of Falling

When you walk to the edge of all the light, and you have to take that first step into the darkness of the unknown, you must believe that one of two things will happen: There will be something solid for you to stand upon, or you will be taught to fly.

– PATRICK OVERTON

After a few days in Guiones, we decided to head to Arenal—one of the tallest active volcanos in Central America. The drive to reach Arenal snaked around the large volcanic lake. It took us about four and a half hours without a functioning radio in the rental vehicle. Stephen enjoyed practicing his driving techniques by accelerating into the tight curves and hugging the edges of the nonexistent lanes on newly paved roads. As a former motocross champion, he knew what he was doing, but I couldn't bring myself to look up. I was so nervous I sipped from a tiny Jack Honey bottle in the glove box and nervously ate all of the nibbles we had packed for the trip.

The hotel was a pleasant surprise—our Expedia half-price special was beautiful. One of the chalet's walls was made of glass and faced the giant volcano. We took a walk around the hotel grounds to familiarize ourselves. Haze hung thick in the air but the forecasted rain held off, so we decided to drive to La Fortuna for dinner. Our first stop was the chocolate store for a few pieces to tide me over while we decided on dinner. Like the Snickers candy bar commercial, I reached a point about every three to four hours where if food wasn't involved, things didn't go so well. If a guy wanted to date me, my priorities were made clear up front: He had better be packin'—snacks, that is.

We found a spot, the Mango Tree Bar, nearby—a local restaurant with a giant tree growing through its middle and out the rooftop. The bar had female wrestling on one TV, old wrestling footage of Andre the Giant on the second TV, and soccer on the third. We laughed about watching wrestling as kids, and I recalled my dad taking my sister and me to Louisville Gardens Arena to a couple of matches. Bill Dundee was her favorite and I loved Jerry "The King" Lawler. I ordered a much-anticipated cocktail after surviving the curves for hours. I had no idea how to pronounce it or what it contained, but gave it a shot nonetheless. Stephen continued his foreign beer experiment by ordering a couple of local brews.

At the end of a long day, we were beat. We started a tradition of taking time for a slow dance each night before bed—less because we were being romantic and more because there was nothing else to do at the condo. The only music we had was whatever was already on my laptop. We took turns playing DJ each night, and it ended up being one of the things I most looked forward to. We felt at peace and grateful to be in those moments.

It was a rare luxury to watch the one English-speaking channel that evening at bedtime. I was happy to have been missing all the political noise at home, but occasionally, it was nice to see what was happening in the worlds where the money is made. We took advantage of having Wi-Fi in the hotel room and played music from YouTube for our evening dance. Norah Jones' rendition of "Tennessee Waltz" seemed fitting for two Nashvillians. So, we capped off our night with a moonlit dance beside the volcano.

We awoke the next day just after sunrise and in through the massive window shone a breathtaking view of the volcanic setting without a single cloud—only slips of smoke piping from the hot lava beneath the surface at its peak. I sat at breakfast and inhaled the view of blue sky, red and yellow birds and butterflies, and intoxicating green plants surrounding the lagoon between the restaurant and volcano. It felt too perfect to be real.

That feeling of bliss triggered flashbacks to some of the previously endured "shoulds," because I fled from them rather than filtering them. Relationships with men in the past brought deep pain and, I guess, at that point on this journey I was in touch enough with my emotions to feel it. There was ducking clear of the sedan driven by the church elder-turned-stalker. Oh, and those hideous pink lace bridesmaid dresses. (I didn't like pink, but it matched the church décor chosen by the family.) Any vision of planning my own wedding, wearing that purple dress, riding on horses, or choosing my fate vanished. I wore an off-white dress because it wouldn't have been appropriate to wear a white one, being that I was more than four months pregnant. I ate KFC mashed potatoes with a spork from within a stall in the church bathroom to settle my stomach while stubbornly refusing to allow tears to mess up my painted-on face. Resigning to the Should Monster's heavy grasp … *The show must go on.*

The fear of entrapment came rushing in and hot tears threatened to manifest while I asked for the key so I could exit without having to materialize those thoughts with words. Now recognizing the fact that all that time I already had the power to push back, the apprehension crept up before I could stop it. Stephen sensed something was wrong and pulled it out of me. I didn't want our trip to end. I didn't want to leave this natural beauty. I didn't want to return home and become consumed by busyness as an excuse to avoid feeling love. Going back to being my old self was a horrifying thought.

Everything felt fleeting and that old familiar sense of panic welled up in my heart as the Should Monster whispered, *Run. Ignore this man. He will change. This feeling won't last. Don't trust him. Don't put yourself out there; you'll only get hurt.* I have to give Stephen credit. He held my hand, gently asked me to stay at the table, and tell him what was wrong. He understood. He leaned over and kissed my cheek softly and promised those days were over, that we control our own destinies, and that he loved me. I didn't know whether to kiss him back or run away even faster. I finished breakfast in silence. Frozen with fear at the thought of being truly loved. *Was it even possible?*

Our last day near Arenal, we visited La Fortuna Waterfall. We missed the turn-off point three different times and were frustrated by the time we finally arrived. We paid the park admission and headed full out down the third-of-a-mile of well-groomed steps to view the falls in all their glory. The day prior, we met some tourists from Vancouver who suggested we investigate an old, hidden trail across the river at the bottom of the falls. Of course, we wanted to check it out.

The same rainstorm that removed haze from the volcano created dangerous crossing conditions. We removed our shoes and carefully zigzagged from slick boulder to boulder as the rapids ran beneath. My sunglasses were swept off and down the river by a crashing surge of water. Luckily, everything else made it safely during the 15-minute river crossing. We quickly found the hidden trail off the beaten path behind some trees. It had a 100-year-old set of rock-and-concrete-lain steps, wet with moisture from the rainforest and edged with slick moss. We walked through the national park, across the waterfall and up the other side, reaching 1,000 meters at the top. As if that wasn't spectacular enough, there was an abandoned zipline tie-off platform of grated, slotted metal that emerged another 75 feet above the peak atop the tree canopy.

Of course, we climbed it. I literally clung to the railing at the top of the steps while Stephen took photos of the view. Climbing that type of steps always made me nervous—as a child when we visited Mammoth Cave National Park, I slid through the middle of the open slots between the steps. Luckily, my mother quickly grabbed my arm and kept me from falling deep into the cavern pit beneath. As an adult, I forced myself to go up that design of stairway to face the fear, rationalizing with myself at each rung, *Everybody uses these. They're safe. Don't be a sissy.*

Happy to have gotten some photos of the canopy and waterfall far beneath us, Stephen was ready to make our way back. We began descending the hand-hewn, moss-covered rock steps. This trail was not part of the national park, so safety standards were minimal, and it was very slick. We usually did a fast walk or slow jog on short hikes like this, but we were meeting another group that was ascending the steps, so we were walking cautiously on the outside of the walkway. During this particular stretch, right after passing the 600-meter marker, there was a chain rope just above waist high to signal the steep drop off.

Before the gasps could exit the lips of the tourists, my right foot stepped directly on a wet mossy patch and slid uncontrollably off the ledge. The weight of my entire body flew fully underneath the chain and dangled off the cliff. Luckily, I had my right hand loosely on the chain and instinctively gripped it upon falling. My body hung like a rag doll from a shoulder that was obviously out of socket. One of the men coming up the other direction grabbed my left arm and yanked me to safety within seconds. Stephen turned around at the sound of the commotion and leapt up the steps between us, but by that time it was already over.

That's the closest I've come to staring death in the face. (*What was it with me and steps, anyway?!*) I shook it off with some sort of monkey-armed joke, apologized to passersby for interrupting their hike, and we continued down the trail. After about 100 meters, Stephen made me stop for a bit to assess injuries. The shoulder hurt, and there were a few gashes down my backside from banging against the rocky cliff, but I assured him it would be fine. I had always been able to dislocate my shoulders. Sometimes as a kid, if we were bored at school, I'd use those gross contortion skills to get a few laughs and provide a distraction.

This was one time it was fortunate to be monkey-like. My tailbone had smacked against the rocky bluff and hurt, but wasn't broken. My legs shook uncontrollably at the realization that if my hand hadn't been on that chain, if the stranger hadn't grabbed me so quickly ... I've never experienced shaking like that before and convinced Stephen we should just walk it off. That's what Scotts do—we suck it up and move on until the pain stops. It seemed to work. I tried not to think about what could have been if I had dropped off the cliff and to focus on keeping one foot in front of the other, moving forward.

Upon reaching the rapids to enter back into the national park, we found a shallower part downstream to cross. I removed my hiking shoes and tiptoed across in a matter of minutes. Stephen decided he wanted to attempt making it across without removing his shoes and deliberated various potential paths for well over 15 minutes before finally beginning his climb across. I gave up waiting for him and went upstream a bit to watch local families splashing about in a lagoon area beneath the rapids.

Finally, Stephen emerged with face lit up like a kid in a candy store. His wrist looked as if a golf ball had been inserted where the usual bone should have been, and his shin (from knee to ankle) was bright red. He had decided to take a flying leap at the end (which, he said, would either end in a lot of pain or the glory of not getting his shoes wet). He landed on the slick rock and slid mercilessly into the water. Shoes saturated and his body clearly injured, he was still happy for the adventure and to have not been swept down the rapids. We made our way to the same third-of-a-mile-long set of steps leading back up to the parking lot. In typical form, I made eye contact with Stephen at the foot of the busy stairway and despite everything that had happened that day, gave him the unmistakable look. He knew what I was saying without words: *Wanna race?*

So we did. A competitive tennis athlete, Stephen was more powerful and shot up the first several flights at break-neck speed. My theory was to do a paced, but exerted run, thinking he would wear out near the top. He's an obnoxious competitor. Seriously. That kind man turns into a barracuda when competition is involved. Literally shoving small kids, old ladies, and anyone else aside with his ape-like arms as he barked, "Hey! ... Move!" I tried to keep up and laughed the whole time at the absurdity of two injured fortysomethings racing straight up 530 stairs after hiking, dangling off a cliff, and slipping into the river. Towards the top, Stephen's pace finally slowed, and I came within 15 steps of him, but couldn't catch up. This man was crazy. So was I. It felt great. I tried out the same technique Kay had used on my knee to help Stephen's wrist return to about *half* the size of a golf ball while he navigated the winding roads back to Guiones. He knew about the energy-healing techniques I had studied but had not experienced their effects personally until that day. Stephen returned to the States a week after that.

I thought a lot about what believing in love meant. My perspective shifted. Love is much greater than just a romance. It's the feeling of true appreciation for nature, for beauty, for a favorite food, and for other humans. It's appreciating that we can give it away without condition, even to those with whom we vehemently disagree. Love is knowing when to let go and when to hang on. I realized through this experience that we get to invent our own definition of love and that embracing it fully empowers us. For me, having a play friend at this point in time was perfect. I recognized the "shoulds" from others about relationships were not for me. Kay was right. The best rewards come from the heart.

After Stephen left, I painted another butterfly and a couple other birds we saw on our travels, finishing the 11 thank-you cards painted during the trip. I certainly had a lot for which to be grateful. My daily routines resumed back in Guiones at the beach, bluffs, and jungle trails there. I even took a couple of swimming lessons; it was something I'd always wanted to learn to do so I could sign up for a triathlon someday. Each day, more vivid dreams, more connected experiences, and more intuition flowed forth than at any time in my life. And I was taking time to journal it all, something I'd never done before—just taking time to do many things that made me feel excited to be alive.

There was nothing special making me feel this way. I still didn't have a job or a plan. I didn't have a lot of possessions to return to, and even my relationship with Stephen was a day-by-day adventure without any thoughts for an extended future. And yet, there it was, this ongoing euphoria of being full of the Spirit and of love and of gratitude just for being alive in each minute. It wasn't dependent on anything. This joy was not a result of things happening to me—it came from within me like an endless fountain, like being on some crazy natural high.

Buttress Tree in Nosara Jungle

CHAPTER 21

9° North

Platypus: A platypus bill is comprised of thousands of cells that give it a sixth sense, allowing it to detect electric fields generated by all living things. It's so sensitive that the platypus can hunt with its eyes, ears, and nose all closed relying entirely on its bill's electrolocation.

No bug piles outside my door this morning—only the usual dozens of insects climbing the walls, walking across the ceiling, and scuttling along the floors throughout the little Costa Rican condo. The daily wake-up routine had begun. Crush creepy crawlers with flip-flops, scoot tiny bugs off the kitchen countertop, then make coffee. It felt incredible to be alive and unbitten!

I reached the jungle trail where the alpha monkey, Samson, wept with me weeks ago and began my daily run with hope that fatigue would undress any final buried memories. Running had become my primary solace during the last 10 years. The rhythmic, mindless movement and resulting exhaustion predictably changed my focus from the stress and anxiety at hand into simply thinking about what type of food I should devour afterwards. This day, I wasn't running from anything, I was just celebrating all the energy from inside as my time in this magical place was nearing its end.

Running was different with the scorching heat, vine-filled passages, and steep hills of the jungle here at 9° north of the equator. Having greeted the usual welcoming committee of coatimundi a couple miles into the sweltering forest, I realized I had forgotten to remove my outer shirt. The trusty dust shield had been my most reliable garment during the trip—originally white and now a lovely muddled, earthy color. I paused to tie my tried-and-true thin, long-sleeved cotton shirt gently to the branch of a tree before continuing.

It's difficult to explain the energy in this place—the oneness with nature—I would surely miss it. I felt it in my bones with every bird babble, reptile rustle, and plant prick along the path. It's the goosebumps you get from an impossibly beautiful song, the anticipation felt as your sports team takes the field for the big game, and the subconscious humming that occurs when eating your favorite home-cooked meal. It's more like a bouncy bluegrass ditty than a solemn sonata. I loved feeling that energy of the jungle, running through its tangled greenery and among its lively animals.

I made it to the trail's turnaround point and started back to the car where nourishing stocks of water and nuts awaited. It was important to carry a bottle of water in each hand, even for just a few miles of running, because the intense heat quickly causes dehydration. On the route back, I remembered my shirt. I had already passed where it was placed and turned around to retrieve it, thinking maybe I'd missed it.

My two bottles of water were already depleted, as I hadn't planned for additional miles. The sun would set by the time I went all the way to the car for replenishment and staying in the jungle at night was not an option. It was rare enough to be a female out alone in this remote area of Costa Rica, but add to that being surrounded by wild animals, and the odds of spending a safe, cozy night on the trail were nil.

Traveling an extra mile up steep terrain, I did not see the shirt where it was left. I was getting lightheaded from dehydration and heat. I decided to forget about the shirt and focus on making it back safely to the trailhead before the sun sank further. I slowed from jogging to slowly walking to conserve energy, and panic started to creep in. The unnerving thing about walking instead of jogging is you not only *hear* the lizards and snakes whooshing away from the trail, sometimes you can *feel* them.

I prayed out loud, as I'd become accustomed to in this jungle. No more fear of what others may think about my dialogue with the Spirit, or the animals, or especially myself. "Lord, I know this was a dumb mistake. My water is empty. I am alone in the jungle, and I just want to find my trusty overshirt. Just send me a sign to help me know where it is, OK? Oh, but *please* nothing scary like the scorpions or snakes again. How about a nice … duck?" To be honest, I didn't know if there were ducks in this part of the Costa Rican jungle, I was just trying to think in an instant of a creature in the wild that would not be frightening. There had been enough of that lately.

About 10 minutes later, and still no sign of the shirt, a squatty duck-like creature—*was it a platypus?*—scrambled right in front of me and went up into the woods honking. Aware of this manifestation, I laughed so loud that it brought Samson, the alpha male monkey who had become my favorite conversationalist, down from the treetops. The bizarreness of it all—*Who am I to have this dialogue with the Spirit?*

I followed the little platypus-looking creature (which actually turned out to be a native wood-rail) about half the length of a football field off the trail. There laid my shirt at the intersection of a low-hanging branch and the trunk of a mighty buttress tree. The monkeys must have taken it off of the tree where I left it and transported it near their home base. Instead of the typical, roaring howler-monkey warning, Samson gave me a resounding grunt-like "Oor, oor, oor!" message—perhaps his way of laughing. He had successfully carried out his mischief.

I'd be lying if I said I wasn't incredibly scared. He and his troop could maul me in a heartbeat—there could be an army of them at his beck and call in the canopy above. I was alone. He could throw something at me, like a nut or, even worse, some poo. But he just grunted, or laughed. This was the same frightening, curious, and playful guy who wept with me weeks ago as I left my past alongside the dried up leaves on the forest floor.

What were you supposed to say to an alpha monkey? "Look what a good boy you are! You took my shirt, you sneaky guy. Good boy. Thank you." He grunted eagerly. Still in a bit of disbelief and marveling that this unexpected duck-platypus creature led me to the monkeys' hiding spot, I gave a few well-intended grunts back, cautiously retrieved my shirt, and returned to the trail. Never in my life had I interacted so intimately with such wild animals. This was a special place. I felt compelled to acknowledge out loud at that moment, "I don't care how high the hill, I will climb it. I will serve, go, do, preach, write, teach, heal—whatever I feel led to do. I am not afraid to take the risk." The jungles have a way of changing us—of scaring us, fascinating us, drawing us in, and spitting us out. I thought to myself, *Take the risk. Shed your skin. Ignite your power. You've got this.*

That final journal entry detailing the last traipse through the jungle fell at the end of Guiones' dry season. After six long months of drought, the spring rains began to pound the parched earth, and the plants and animals came alive with gratitude. Green fronds happily wriggled open, the cows became fat again, and the season of surviving and conserving energy within was over. Now it was time to thrive. And I was prepared to continue following my animal instincts as I headed home full of love, power, and purpose. I wanted to share what I learned with others. It didn't require a trip to the jungle, a fancy process, or a series of elaborate rituals to reconnect with my personal Inner Owl. The Light was there my entire life—it just needed to be set free to shine into the world again.

Persistence

CHAPTER 22

Embrace Your Own Animal Instincts

Tabitha: Derived from the Aramaic word for "gazelle";
also a Hebrew name meaning "grace"

Gazelle: Most gazelles live in the hot, dry savannas and
deserts of Africa and Asia. To stay hydrated in these grueling
environments, gazelles shrink their heart. A smaller heart needs
less oxygen, so the animal can breathe less and conserve water.
Gazelles rely on their speed to escape from predators.
As one of the fastest animals, they run up to 60 mph.

Upon returning home, I reflected on the things experienced and learned in the jungle. I thought about my true self. A natural klutz, my friends will attest I am not graceful like the gazelle. I did, however, shrink my heart for many years to escape fear, pain, and predators. While it helped me survive short term, it created burnout and imbalance over the years. I ran from the monsters of the modern jungle but eventually learned the freedom I sought was achieved most quickly by standing still, unwavering within the beliefs from my own soul.

It became evident that we are each born with this fiery spirit. We cry, we search for nourishment, and we fight to survive. We crawl, we walk, and eventually we leap and run. We sometimes allow the "shoulds" to paralyze us with fear. I've got news for you: We can choose to not be afraid. We are not alone and we don't need anyone else's permission to embrace our whole hearts and to drink from the renewable fountain of life. Our lights in the world are a God-given source of energy and power that we own, that we *are*.

My life changed a lot upon returning home from Guiones. I completed my first triathlon. Like an uncomfortable, panicky cat in the water, I learned just enough from lessons overseas and subsequent practice to get myself halfway through the 400-meter swimming portion of the race using the proper technique before having to flip over and finish with an ugly mash-up of backstroke meets puppy paddle.

My house eventually sold, and I moved into a small condo in the city. I had everything I needed—a bed, a sofa, my grandma's old purple velvet chair, the incredible paintings and glass sculptures created by Ethan, and a gorgeous, modern Nashville skyline photo taken by Trent's drone that was stretched across a giant canvas. With his love for diving, wildlife, and the environment, Ethan became a glass-blowing instructor and moved to St. Louis where his beautiful artwork raises awareness for coral-reef restoration. In addition to having his pilot's license, Trent became a Master Scuba Diver and began teaching personal protection and gun safety. And I got a new baby—a baby grand piano, that is. After living in a home for decades without one, I reveled in having the opportunity to play music again. Rusty from not feeling the vibes for so long, the melodies inside soon returned and spilled out through my fingers onto the keys.

I wrapped up the practicum required for the final level of energy-healing certification, and separately completed credentials to administer and consult on the European-based AEM-Cube, a tool based on systems theory and ethology (change) that identifies how people are energized in different ways. While seemingly unrelated, the education from both equipped me with better tools to help people identify and tap into their own potential and purpose. I put my passion into action by hosting a symposium for strategic diversity that brought together Fortune 500 companies, government officials, and industry experts to identify ways to support all types of diversity and inclusion.

And, I took a job with an ambiguous title at a large retailer head-quartered in the Nashville area. For the first time in 20 years there were no officer letters following my name. It felt great to have a role I could emotionally leave at the door, while leaning into my new life game—that fulfilling purpose we invent and reinvent, over time, to stay in sync with our learning, passions, and changes in perspective. This job was an opportunity to share my gifts, to support others, to observe energy dynamics in the workplace, and to practice maintaining a high-vibrational state.

I continued to give keynotes and workshops, but instead of the focus being only on how to increase shareholder wealth, the topics expanded to helping people power their own potential. If a company's leadership and team members are energized by and are passionate about what they do, profits follow. I introduced the Should Monster and Inner Owl concepts to audiences and was encouraged to share my personal journey, lessons learned, and ideas in this book. My audiences expanded from groups of C-Suite executives, government officials, university scholars, and tech leaders to also include women's organizations, employee resource groups, and faith-based groups.

I decided to write this book and reveal the triumphs and tribulations of my personal transformation, fully understanding the risk of exposing myself as a vulnerable student of the universe instead of the got-it-together executive image that used to be so important to me. I let go of that fear and embraced the opportunity to serve others. Everyone can enjoy recharging their life and reconnecting to intuition and vibrant, joyful energy.

It doesn't matter what your religion, political party, ethnicity, race, economic status, or personal preferences are. They don't control or define your spirit, your intuition, or the shared energy pulsing through our physical bodies because we all have identical access. It doesn't matter if the Should Monster says you'll look silly. It's *your* potential to tap into, to embrace, to love, and to share. So, go ahead. Take the risk. Ignite your power.

.

PART 3
Powering Potential

Arenal Volcano in La Fortuna

CHAPTER 23

Belief Drives Everything

If I have the belief that I can do it, I shall surely acquire the capacity to do it even if I may not have it at the beginning.

– MAHATMA GANDHI

I believe in both the science and spiritual aspects of energy, and my current life game is to help people and companies discover and ignite their untapped potential. Therefore, this section shifts from the "what" (shed harmful pressures, reconnect, and protect your own power) to the "why" and "how" (why science's energy is the same as spiritual energy, why high-vibrational spiritual energy is worth it, and techniques to raise and maintain your vibration). Although I've spent many years studying electrical and human energy, I am an evolving student—work in progress. It is with great humility that I present these ideas with a full understanding there are many complementary sources of knowledge that I will continue to explore to keep growing and expanding these concepts over time.

Based on the experience I have, as of the writing of this book, I assert that our *beliefs* drive everything. Beliefs are our way of focusing our energy to bring our thoughts and desires into reality. The concept is prevalent in both ancient religions and modern psychology.

I respectfully reference the physical laws and energetic concepts throughout this book as a layperson and these citations are not meant to imply that I have advanced degrees in physics or psychology—I do not. While the assertions herein have been reviewed by several experts, this content is intended to reinforce the similarities in characteristics between human behavior, spirituality, and universal energetic scientific truths, and to proclaim that these scientific truths reinforce the existence of a universal, all-knowing Spirit, or energy source, that is omnipresent among and within us all equally.

Our physical bodies, mental states, and actions are manifestations of our beliefs. Prolific evidence about the power of belief is being leveraged in many new and positive ways, like helping wounded military service members eliminate the use of opioids. In *National Geographic*'s 2016 edition about the science of healing, we discover how patients' bodies physically reacted to a known placebo of their choosing, such as a peppermint, as if they had ingested the actual prescription drug itself. (The placebo effect is an improvement in a patient's condition that cannot be attributed to a particular treatment itself, and must, instead, occur in response to their *belief* in that particular type of treatment.)

According to neuroscientist Fabrizio Benedetti, one of the pioneers of placebo research, fake painkillers can also trigger the release of natural pain-relieving chemicals called endorphins. Patients with Parkinson's disease respond to placebos with a flood of dopamine. Fake oxygen, given to someone at altitude, has been shown to cut levels of neurotransmitters called prostaglandins, which dilate blood vessels, among other things, and are responsible for many of the symptoms of altitude sickness. How is this possible when the placebos themselves, which are by definition inert, are not the cause of the improved condition? The positive reaction is instead triggered by our *belief* in the treatments. Our expectation that *we will feel better* is as powerful a force as the drug itself, substantiating the validity of natural healing techniques. Perhaps my belief in the possibility of having a meaningful transformation while in Costa Rica actually opened the door for it to occur.

An ancient and well-documented demonstration of the effectiveness of belief is prayer. Prayer is the act of focusing our energy with the belief that it will produce an intended outcome. It is used to bless food, bring relief, carry on conversations with the Spirit, set intentions, release guilt, forgive others, and a number of other purposes. Another example of belief is the use of positive visualization for training or practice by athletes, businesspeople, or performers to mentally rehearse successful scenarios in advance. This mental focus of energy improves the likelihood of performing well, whether it's mentally rehearsing a monologue, a job interview, the perfect swimming technique, or a complex chord progression for a recital.

The three most important areas of belief needed to tap into our energetic sources of wisdom and connectivity are belief in the Spirit, belief in self, and belief in love.

"The same energy that powers the universe is the lifeblood of all things, including you and me."

-Tabitha A. Scott

The Golden Spiral

CHAPTER 24

Belief in the Spirit: The Universal Power of Life

One life is all we have and we live it as we believe in living it.
But to sacrifice what you are and to live without belief,
that is a fate more terrible than dying.

– JOAN OF ARC

The "Spirit" in the context of this book is the overall, universal source of power (energy). It is quite real and is scientifically proven to exist in many forms. Just as the eye cannot see electricity flowing through power lines, yet it illuminates the light in our homes, the Spirit flows infinitely as the essence of all living things. It provides the "life-light" for experiencing our current state of awareness. I capitalize Spirit to distinguish it from other forms of spirits, such as those who have transitioned from this lifetime, animals, or our own inner voice. It is also to show honor and respect to various cultural and religious beliefs—we are speaking about *the* highest source of truth, wisdom, and power.

Since mankind's earliest days, we have described this energy source in many ways, such as through gods, legends, elements of the Earth, numbers, astrology, and stories. Over half the world's population today believes in a monotheistic God. They believe God is omnipresent and available in Spirit form to serve as a source of wisdom, love, guidance, and compassion. Further, the Spirit is believed to provide extraordinary powers, allowing those who *believe* to exceed their perceived potential, often referred to as "miracles." Raised in the Christian faith, we called it the Holy Spirit. The Holy Spirit reference appears 389 times in the Old Testament and in 261 passages in the New Testament of the Bible, so belief in the Spirit is clearly an important part of Christianity.

Beyond ancient religions, there are many modern-day advocates of the universal energy source or Spirit. One of my favorites, because of his physical and spiritual approach, is Indian Yogi, author, and Special Consult to the United Nations, Sadhguru. In his book *Inner Engineering*, he describes the ultimate resource of energy as the "Intelligence" and also shares many ways to tap into it. Sadhguru teaches that it doesn't matter what you call that universal energy source, but it is fundamental to recognize its power and accessibility. I also appreciate many of the teachings of Deepak Chopra, who has bravely withstood great criticism for comparing human healing to quantum mechanics. His work has inspired millions.

The New Age concept of the Law of Attraction is popular in the U.S. Esther (Abraham) Hicks and Gabrielle Bernstein are among its leading authors and proponents. Simply put, the Law of Attraction is the ability to attract into our lives whatever holds our focus. It is believed that regardless of age, nationality, or religious preference, there is an infinite supply of love and energy from which to partake. While I have yet to find laws of physics that reinforce this methodology, it does assert there is an ultimate source of power that we may all universally access. What I call Spirit, they typically refer to as the Universe. The authors' teachings also reinforce the power of belief. Where our mind goes first, reality manifests next.

People have been trying to tap into the Spirit for millennia, even erecting temples in geographical areas that possess certain energetic attributes. For example, the magnetic equator flows directly through India. The *magnetic* equator is different than the equator of a rotating sphere (which is the circle of latitude found around the middle of its two poles); the magnetic equator (represented in the following graphic as the dotted line) is an

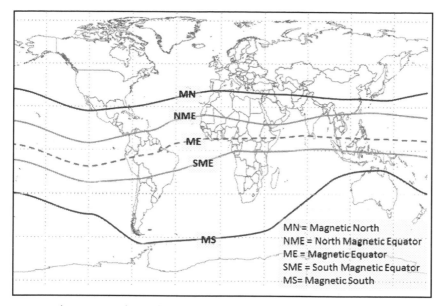

MN = Magnetic North
NME = North Magnetic Equator
ME = Magnetic Equator
SME = South Magnetic Equator
MS= Magnetic South

Source: https://www.iasparliament.com/current-affairs/daily-news/isros-path-to-100th-satellite-launch

imaginary, connected line representing the area of the earth's magnetic field that is entirely neutral. In other words, there is no pull of magnetism in one way or the other. Temples were built along the magnetic equator because its properties provide the least possible energetic interference between our human biofields and the earth's own biofields. Interestingly, the location I visited in Costa Rica lies very close to the North Magnetic Equator line, as demonstrated in the graphic below. I wonder if that is one of the reasons why I seemed to experience less interference, and greater balance, while connecting from there.

Since this book already describes in detail how we are vibrating, energetic beings who are subject to the laws and properties of energy itself, I won't repeat it all again here. It is worth reiterating, however, that everything from our economics, sociology, and musical pitch to the manifestation of rocks, trees, animals, and our own bodies are simply variations of energy frequencies. Every living cell has its own healthy frequency and all living things (including organizations) share the same life cycle or growth curve—birth, growth, maturity, and decline.

And remember, lower frequencies represent more basic physical and psychological needs like eating and basic social acceptance; while higher frequencies are used for more complex physical or psychological states like imagination, self-actualization, yoga, and connectedness to the Spirit.

Energy, as the Spirit, is the source of everything and the ultimate renewable resource that can recharge us mentally, physically, and spiritually. This is the foremost epiphany placed within my heart that I am passionate about sharing with others. It pains me to hear people arguing about what to call it, which religion is the "right" one, or feeling like we, as humanity, are alone in this vast universe. This Spirit is here for you, for me, for all of us. It doesn't cost anything, and anyone can accept and leverage its power, without agenda.

Intelligent Intuition

CHAPTER 25

Belief in Self: Your Personal Reconnection to Power

The thing always happens that you really believe in;
and the belief in a thing makes it happen.

– FRANK LLOYD WRIGHT

By "self," I am referring to the specific, individual source of energy within us. By "believing" I mean to practice forgiving ourselves, being champions for ourselves, allowing ourselves to stay open and take risks, and treating ourselves to things that foster well-being and happiness. These practices elevate our positivity and allow us to participate in high-vibrational activities. Applying nonjudgmental, unconditional love to yourself also makes it easier to share that same pure love with others.

It takes a lot of courage to believe in yourself, to stand up for your own needs and wants, and to believe that you can shape the future you desire deeply enough that you will take the risk—even if it's scary or intimidating—to attain your dreams. Like the death-before-battle samurai technique I used to face my fear of defeating the Should Monster in the jungle, ask yourself, "What's the *worst* thing that can happen?" Remember failure helps us reach our goals because it shows us what doesn't work,

179

allowing us to redirect focus to other possible alternatives. Viewing failure as a positive, natural part of progress, rather than something negative, is a powerful way of believing in ourselves. The realization that nothing is truly good or bad, that we have the power to assign all meaning, gives us the freedom to find joy in the events of the present and to let go of the past. Believing in self is about leveraging our personal connection to the Spirit's potential. Physical advantages are easy to spot: the 7-foot-tall basketball player, the hyper-flexible gymnast, and the swimmer with a long torso (and mastery of the proper technique!) all have it easier within their chosen sport. Individual spiritual potential, however, is the great equalizer. Humans are all 100-percent equally capable of accessing and growing our innate connections to the Spirit. How exciting is that?!

Tuning In to the Spirit's Resource

STAY OPEN AND RECEPTIVE

To get in touch with our own intuition, belief exponentially accelerates the process. To discover my own Inner Owl, if you recall, I asked the universe during meditation or just prior to bed at night and then listened with an open mind and heart. Opening myself in this way, that was counter to my previous logic-based way of thinking, required *belief*, a leap of faith that the Spirit would return an answer while I remained receptive to it.

Your intuition, or animal instinct, may not appear as an actual Great Horned Owl at your window like mine did, but it made sense for me as I've always connected to animals. Perhaps it will come as another spirit animal, an inner voice, a beautiful flower, an unusual cloud, a feeling, or an art form. The ways we connect to our intuition are personal and custom-tailored for each person. And give it time and patience. Remember, the Spirit answered my request for an animal guide, but even though I thought I was being receptive, it took many interactions with the owl and an external person's help to finally decode the message and properly tune in. Over time, with patience and practice, the ability to tune in improves.

Listening to our own intuition may be tough amidst the increasing distractions of the world. It's not a one-size-fits-all approach, as there are as many unique frequencies for tuning in as there are human beings on our planet. While recognizing your intuition will be singular to your experiences, I realized clues to mine included a gut feeling, goosebumps, humming subconsciously, long-overdue tears, and the animals and people that showed up around me.

Self-Regulate: Amplifiers & Insulators

Tapping into your own Inner Owl—or whatever animal, voice, or image represents your intuition—does not require a trip to the jungle. Igniting our personal potential, or tuning in to our intuition, requires three steps, which we'll explore in greater detail in later chapters:

- Identify and filter out the Should Monster and other harmful forces in your life.
- Avoid, redirect, or let go of negative energy (lower vibrations) to protect your positive energy.
- Believe in the Spirit, in yourself, and in love to reconnect and amplify positive energy (higher vibrations).

Navigating those three steps provides a map to our spiritual connectedness, and we must do so very mindfully. Realizing that around 90 percent of the things we do every day are habits, we must alter daily behaviors to avoid burnout, depression, and anxiety. We must increase activities that amplify our positive vibrations and decrease those that insulate it, so that we can more easily connect with our intuition. While the purpose of this book is to introduce the concepts of our energetic state and that its optimization is the source of personal fulfillment, it is not intended as a one-size-fits-all approach. Rather, I share the amplifiers and insulators identified from my own life experiences, and encourage you to create your own unique list.

Here are some of the methods I used to amplify the voice of my Inner Owl. These activities may also raise your energetic vibration, resulting in feelings of happiness, contentment, enthusiasm, and positivity. Some of the practices are: meditation (which can include prayer, yoga, art, or being immersed in nature), gratitude, hiking, cycling, riding horses, playing an instrument, or listening to your favorite music. Each technique identified that elevates your positive vibrations will make it easier to hear your intuition, those messages from the Spirit. Our vibes, both positive and negative, are invisible, yet we can actually often feel them. For example, if we see a photo of a snake coiled and ready to strike, we feel a type of fear in our gut. On the contrary, gazing at adorable kitten or baby photos may incite feelings of hope or joy.

Albert Einstein asserts, "Everything in life is a vibration." Another famous physicist, Erwin Schrödinger, writes, "I insist upon the view that all is waves." Both perspectives reinforce the notion that our ontological state of being oscillates between positive and negative energies; it ripples back and forth like the ebb and flow of the sea, giving us the energetic capacity to generate greater positivity (high-vibration activities) or greater negativity (low-vibration activities).

When discussing this attribute with a friend, we agreed it's how we may explain music to be such a soulful body filler. While I'm not sure the Beach Boys understood the physics behind their hit song "Good Vibrations," the physics of music is fundamentally about waves. Whether longitudinal or transverse, the waves of music have the ability to penetrate solid matter, like vibrating the speakers in the car, or shattering a fine crystal glass, or reaching deep inside our souls to strike a chord of memories, sadness, or elation.

We must also be mindful of insulators, those things that drown out our intuition: over-analyzing, alcohol, food as a distraction, ignoring feelings, commiserating with people who consistently have a negative vibe, and burying ourselves in busyness to avoid our inner selves. Those activities can lower our vibrational state, making it more difficult to hear our intuition.

Make your own list of amplifiers and insulators in your life in the Workbook section of this book or on sticky notes placed in areas that can help remind you to maximize and repeat the amplifiers while you minimize and reduce the insulators. This will improve your optimal energetic balance and help you more easily access your potential.

Intuition Leads to a Sense of Purpose

Finding your own version of the Inner Owl begins with belief. There is a reason "believe in yourself" is at the core of nearly every self-help book—because it's important. By accepting our spiritual power and the joy that comes from giving away unconditional love, we can grow belief in ourselves exponentially. The positive, high vibrations we experience from embracing the Spirit and loving others will help affirm our personal power and trust in ourselves. Sometimes, the Should Monster may try to convince us we're being selfish by listening to our own needs and wants, but taking the risk through action is what ignites the flame of connected purpose.

To use a very clear example, we observe this in people like Martin Luther King Jr.—he believed in the Spirit, himself, love, and the truth of his convictions, and then he took the risk of staring down racial injustice through *action*. Or consider Malala Yousafzai, the Pakistani activist for female education and the youngest Nobel Prize laureate: She didn't just silently believe women deserved equal education rights—she spoke out despite violent Taliban forces opposing her and her ideas. When she learned that she, a young girl, had become a target of the Taliban, she worried about what she would do if confronted with one who wanted to kill her.

On "The Daily Show" with Jon Stewart, she explained, "I said, 'Malala, just take a shoe and hit him.' But then I said, 'If you hit a Talib with your shoe, then there would be no difference between you and the Talib. You must not treat others … with cruelty and harshness. You must fight others, but through peace and through dialogue and through education.' Then I said, 'I'll tell him how important education is and that I even want it for your children as well.' And I will say, 'That is what I want to tell you.

Now do what you want.'" Malala was taking a risk for which she was willing to suffer immensely to amplify the passion she felt in pursuing women's rights. Belief in herself and in her purpose were foundational requirements, but moving her ideas into effectiveness required action, as well.

Finding our purpose can seem daunting but listening, in addition to action, helps. Other advocates of leveraging intuition for decision-making include Jonas Salk who said, "Intuition will tell the thinking mind where to look next," and Ingrid Bergman who said, "You must train your intuition—you must trust the small voice inside you, which tells you exactly what to say, what to decide."

Spending time to reconnect with the natural world and disconnect from distractions like technology, work, or the never-ending to-do list, will improve your receptivity. Can't get outdoors? No worries. A recent study involving 7,500 people by Dacher Keltner, a psychologist from UC Berkeley who collaborated with BBC Earth, proved that watching nature videos provides similar improvements. The wildlife clips increased positive emotions and decreased negative ones, when compared to news, drama, and emotionally neutral footage.

Notice when a strong feeling of affinity or gratitude occurs around a certain animal or during a certain activity, then document and research it to learn more. Record your dreams. Rarely are dreams literal and having documentation helps us piece together what our Inner Owl is telling us. One famous example of receiving spiritual guidance during a dream is from an experience of research scientist James Watson. He was trying to define what the design of DNA was like. After a long period of time where Watson asked himself this question, he had a dream of two intertwined snakes. He interpreted the dream as a representation of the double helix—the foundation for all of life.

We must stop thinking and analyzing long enough to hear that still, small voice inside. I purposefully clarify to stop *thinking*, not necessarily to stop *moving*, because people like me achieve mental tranquility best by being physically active. Everyone experiences intuition in different ways.

Plenty of spiritually inspired folks have written about quiet, cross-legged meditation, but that method does not work as well for me.

While learning to hear my own intuition in the moment, I began to notice what actions triggered it, what it felt like, and how to hear it again. What I learned astounded me. The answers had been inside all along, yet I allowed the busyness and pressures of the world to prevent my listening. The more I dove into the science that reinforces the presence of what we cannot see, the more I became inspired to share this ever-present source of renewable power with others.

Beyond helping in our personal lives, listening to that inner voice boosts professional growth. In fact, many ultra-successful billionaires attribute their success to intuition, like Richard Branson, Oprah Winfrey, Bill Gates, and Elon Musk. Recent studies released in the *Harvard Business Review* also show that following our passion increases the likelihood of success. It's the language of the dollar all over again—this personal potential, this connection to intuition, can make companies a lot more money. It can give them the edge over competitors if they align personal potential strengths with the right role to execute corporate strategy. I have led numerous workshops with live demonstrations for Fortune 500 companies showing, in real time, how including and leveraging diverse strengths improves both productivity and innovation.

Travis Kalanick, CEO of Uber, took great risk when he trusted his gut to implement surge pricing. The controversial move was not well received at first, drawing heavy pushback from the market and even his own leadership team. But Kalanick stuck to his intuition and began modifying the policy to raise prices during peak times. Dynamic pricing became incredibly profitable and is now an accepted aspect of Uber's business, as well as other companies like Disney, which quickly followed suit.

Belief in self is a crucial aspect to powering our potential. It is how we access our unique inner compass, gain answers, and take action that aligns with our own unique purpose in this world.

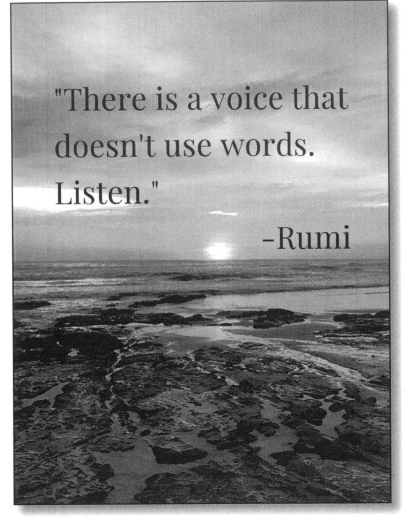

"There is a voice that doesn't use words. Listen."

-Rumi

Rocks on Guiones Beach

CHAPTER 26

Listening to and Trusting Our Intuition

The Universe is not outside of you. Look inside yourself;
everything that you want, you already are.

– RUMI

I believe it is possible for everyone to enjoy the sort of self-actualization described by religious, spiritual, and even modern-day gurus. We just have to identify the ways of tuning in that work for us, then listen to the messages. The stories that follow are true accounts as shared by friends. In some instances, belief in self led to unforeseen positive events; while not listening to personal intuition led to regret. As you read, consider how important trust in intuition is in each of these stories.

Answers behind the Reflection

Beth is a psychologist who grew up in a small Ohio town. Her family was abundant in happiness but limited in financial resources. Her beloved grandmother lived with them and it felt like an idyllic place with family dinners in the evening, a tire swing in the tree out front, and the plump cat, Garfield, who came and went as he pleased. She recalled her childhood home with great fondness, except for two things.

The first was that without the money to build a ramp, Granny was jostled up and down the front porch steps each time the family needed to leave. Her frail frame rattled against the wheelchair as she bravely winced through the painful process. Beth recalls how badly she felt witnessing Granny's transition in and out of the house—often noticing a few tears streaming down her wrinkled cheeks. But the hardship was necessary; the family could not afford to build a ramp.

The second nagging memory was the enormous mirror that hung at the end of the hallway. It was outside Beth's room and looking at it always made her feel unsettled. Everyone in the family disliked the massive, gaudy mirror, but it was firmly attached to the wall when they moved into the home and was too heavy to be easily moved. Instead, they passed it numerous times each day, telling themselves they *should* just ignore the irritating obstacle.

As the years moved on, Granny passed away, and eventually the family relocated. Buyers for the home made the purchase contingent on one thing—removing that ridiculous mirror. Beth remembers the day the movers brought special tools to lift the heavy piece. Behind it was a door leading directly into the driveway. It was an undiscovered path, at ground level, that needed no uncomfortable steps for transition. There was a pile of wood in front of the door on the outside of the home, so although it was there all along, nobody noticed.

This time, the message was in a feeling—literally sensing something for no logical reason. Beth realized, in hindsight, that she and her family had felt their intuition, but unfortunately listened to the Should Monster instead. "We *should* use our time doing something more productive; it would take too much effort and time to remove that gaudy mirror." Not having trusted her intuition and realizing the pain and suffering that could have been prevented was a pivotal point in Beth's life. Today she is highly in touch with her intuition.

The Intersection

It was the winter of 1985 and Bradley had been celebrating with some friends at a party. There was plenty of weed, beer, music, and dancing, and the college students were high on more than life. Bradley was the driver. As he set off from the party with friends in tow, he heard his name spoken from the rear of the car. He stopped and asked his friends, "What?" But no one had spoken. They laughed at him, and he drove on.

A mile or so down the road, a voice so loud and clear it felt as if it was right beside him interrupted the drunken chatter in the car, "Bradley." He heard, but didn't stop, because he thought his friends were messing with him. The car approached East Main Street in Columbus, where the next turn would transition the car and its passengers from a rural road without many cars to a crowded thoroughfare.

As he prepared to turn right onto East Main, he heard, "Bradley, stop!" This time, so certain of the voice and equally certain it did not come from his friends, Bradley pulled into a nearby parking lot and refused to drive further. As he exited the vehicle, the buzz of alcohol and drugs kicked in and he momentarily blacked out—unable to respond for a period of time.

In this case, Bradley's intuition came to him as a voice, undeniably heard and fortunately it was trusted. Now a technology executive at a Fortune 500 Company, Bradley clearly recounted how his Inner Owl saved his own life and the lives of his friends that winter night, perhaps even the fate of others traveling downtown. He never drove under the influence again.

The Birthday Gift

Becky is a counselor and clinical trauma professional with lots of letters after her name (LPC, MHSP, CCTP, CRM, and EMDR). She recounts a cold, rainy day on the 17th of September when she noticed the homeless man, Dockey, who occasionally slept in the garage of the office building where she worked. He was sitting in the usual spot. From time to time, Becky left water bottles for him and once took a blanket to cover him while he slept. That day, she felt a strong urge to give him money.

She recalled, "I thought, *No, I can't give him money because he would probably use it for alcohol, drugs, or something like that*," so she continued on to her office. Becky said her intuition began to tug at her, telling her to give him the money from her purse. It was as if she heard a voice saying, *You should have given him the money. Go back and give it to him.* She reconciled that if he was still there when she returned downstairs for lunch, that she would follow the guidance of the voice.

Upon leaving for lunch, he was still there. Becky looked into her purse and discovered the only cash she had was a $100 bill, which was very rare because she usually carries only a few small bills in cash. She thought, *I surely can't give him $100!* But her heart argued a resounding *Yes, you can.* Becky introduced herself and Dockey said, "Yes ma'am, I've noticed you going in and out of the building before." She handed him the money, and he instantly burst into tears.

That day was Dockey's birthday and he hadn't received a gift in many years. The tearful man retrieved his license to prove it actually was his birthday. The two stood and talked together for a while, and as Becky turned to leave, he asked if he could give her a hug, saying, "You see, you are an angel sent to me today. I cannot give up belief in tomorrow."

Becky was overcome with gratitude for the experience and replied, "No, Dockey, you are a form of God to me today, and I'm happy we have met." She sat numbly in her car before putting it in gear, tears streaming down her cheeks. "I realized at that moment this exchange created a beautiful shift in me, and I began to know the joy of listening to and trusting my inner self, which is undoubtedly connected to a higher Spirit."

These true stories are merely three of untold scores of similar accounts illustrating what happens when we remain open to belief and trust in the messages we receive—resulting in a connection to intuition and the powerful impact it can have on our everyday lives.

Acting on Intuition: Take the Risk

"Hope" is weak. Commitment is powerful. It's not about what you are given or what happens to you; it's about who you are *being* about it. A flood of intuition is useless if we don't *drink in* its wisdom, if we don't live it. Don't stress out if you have to try listening and acting on it a lot before you feel comfortable recognizing the difference between inspiration and analysis. We are trained to conform, not to create, so it may feel awkward at first to "feel" an urge about something and then take the risk to investigate it. Just like with any activity—playing an instrument, painting, or learning a new language—the more you practice building on what *feels* successful, the more finely tuned your intuition will become. We are *all* works in progress and it takes courage to keep improving.

It is of little value to be able to reconnect to the Spirit if we don't take action based on the insights, when appropriate. I'm reminded of an old joke my dad used to tell that demonstrates this concept:

A surge of storms caused an unexpected flood that happened so quickly, residents in low-lying areas scrambled to reach safety. One man named Joe climbed to the second floor of his home to escape the rising waters. The flooding continued and he nervously climbed out the attic windows onto the rooftop. Joe was a man of faith. He believed that what he prayed for in earnest would be granted. From the roof he called out to God, "Lord, it's your humble servant, Joe. I need a miracle and quick! I need you to get me off this rooftop and to safety ..." But his prayer was interrupted by a neighbor who approached in his small fishing boat, yelling loudly to be heard over the gurgling rush of water, "Hey Joe, need any help?"

Joe motioned the neighbor onward, "No thanks, I'm hoping for a miracle." Then, he resumed his prayer, "I believe You will lift me into safety and off of this roof, oh Lord. My hope is in You ..." Again, Joe is interrupted, but this time by a local Coast Guard member, "Hey Mister, take this life preserver until I can deliver this load of people and come back for you."

Annoyed at the second interruption to his prayer, Joe motions the Coast Guard member to keep moving. "No thanks, I believe God is sending me help." He continued to pray for another 30 minutes. The water rose around him and Joe gasped for his final breath as the raging current ultimately swept him under its mighty grasp. Upon arriving in Heaven, Joe asked the Lord, "I'm glad to be here and all, but I don't understand. Your word says if only we believe, we shall receive. I prayed in earnest. I had hope and faith, but why did You let me drown amidst the storm?"

The Lord looked lovingly upon Joe and replied, "My dear son, I heard your request and sent both a boat and a life preserver. The answers to your prayer were granted, but you didn't take the risk to accept them. Hope is but aspiration without action."

Connection to your intuition is powerful, energizing, and inspiring, but just hearing it alone won't set you free. The manifestation of joy in abundance only comes with carrying out the message from your own intuition through action. Like Becky giving the money to Dockey or Malala speaking out for women's rights, we must be willing to risk following it, to let go of fear from paradigms, and to go beyond academically considering or psychologically comprehending it to absolutely, ontologically living it. It takes courage to trust and believe in ourselves despite what others might think. Only when we are actively listening to and living out our potential from the Spirit can we truly *be* free.

Ditch the negative past. Many of us have that person from high school we were too afraid to ask for a date or that job offer that came at a time that wasn't convenient but could have led to something great. Maybe we didn't try out for the team we wanted or didn't audition for the community theatre. We didn't travel abroad, instead choosing the educational path someone else wanted for us. We silently allowed the bullying soccer parent to be too harsh with the players, or we looked the other way when our colleague showed up with a black eye at work … the list goes on and on. Perhaps the "could" is equally as unproductive and destructive as the "should." The most powerful potential is unleashed only when we filter out negative messages from the past while paying attention to and bravely acting in accordance with what incites joy, satisfaction, and excitement in the present.

The book, *The Top Five Regrets of the Dying,* includes documentation of many patients over a period of years who were receiving palliative care during the last 12 weeks of their lives. The regrets touch upon being more genuine, not working so hard, expressing one's true feelings, staying in touch with friends, and finding more joy in life. (Bronnie Ware, *The Top 5 Regrets of the Dying* [Hay House].)

We have a choice to live life without regret. It's not easy to step beyond our comfort zone. It's not always obvious to see the metaphoric boats ready to deliver us off the drowning rooftop. It is, however, worth the risk if the feeling produced when we imagine taking the chance produces invigoration while the worst possible outcome is still tolerable. The original definition of "courage" actually aligns less with external battles and more with the strength of our own internal voice: Courage: *Heart (as the seat of emotions), hence spirit, temperament, state of mind (c. 1300).* Listen to your heart, your intuition, and be brave.

Peaceful Power

CHAPTER 27

Belief in Love: Maintaining a High-Vibration Life

It is good to love many things, for therein lies the true strength, and whosoever loves much performs much, and can accomplish much, and what is done in love, is well done.

– VINCENT VAN GOGH

I love bulls and have for as long as I can remember. As a child, I donned t-shirts with them, collected bobble-head bull figurines, and always cheered them on against the matadors on TV. I begged Dad to let me get a bull instead of a horse—to hug him, tame him, and ride him through the pastures. How cool would that be? Mom said it was because I "always did take the bull by the horns," but there is just something about their silent, powerful face, their strong horns, their piercing eyes that has always captivated me. Feeling particularly stressed out a couple years ago when preparing for a strategic diversity symposium I hosted and funded, I ripped out a magazine ad of a bull and put it on my refrigerator to remind myself that I'm the person who chose to tackle things that aren't easy, to "take the bull by the horns." It instantly made me smile despite the stress because it brought back that feeling of love and reminded me sometimes it takes big risks to accomplish something meaningful and electric.

That very afternoon, I received a text from Ethan with the photo of a drawing he had completed in art college, over 500 miles away. "Thought you'd like this bull; it was chosen for class exhibition (where they post it in front of the class like you used to do with our artwork on the fridge when we were kids)." A wave of eerie disbelief rushed over me and I immediately snapped a photo of my bull on the fridge and posted it side-by-side with his image on Facebook, tagging Ethan. It was uncanny how similar the images were, and that my son would feel the urge to text me the bovine rendering the very day I needed it most. I framed the drawing the following year and it still hangs in my home as an instant way to feel the soaring joy of love.

Love is an ongoing connection that transcends space and time. It is a simple way to maintain a high vibration because everyone has experienced it in at least some way, so we can readily identify with the feeling it produces. But love is an ambiguous word at best—used to describe everything from the romantic love of a lifetime to your favorite flavor of ice cream (it's pistachio gelato sitting atop hot brownies and topped with dark-chocolate syrup, in case you are wondering). I love riding my bicycle by the river, love spending time with my friends, love observing the perfection of each flower, love traveling, love helping others … the list could go on for an eternity. By belief in love, I mean believing in the ability to *sustain the enlightened feeling experienced when doing your favorite things by practicing and maintaining a nonjudgmental, open-hearted sense of well-being and happiness towards yourself and others*—whether you like them or not.

There is no greater source of renewable energy and power than by genuinely giving this type of love into the world and accepting it in return. First you must truly give nonjudgmental, open-hearted love to yourself. For some, this takes practice. Unconditional love is among the highest vibrating energies, so it raises your own positivity, and that of those around you. Give and accept it freely to yourself, then to family, friends, strangers, colleagues, public officials, teachers, those you admire, and those you do not understand. It's like a magic penny—the more you spend it, the more you have. Practicing authentic love generates high vibrations, making us feel energized. Other examples of high-vibrational practices include gratitude, appreciation, compassion, and positivity.

We know that belief in the Spirit, in yourself, and in love helps reconnect us to our intuition and amplifies our high-vibrational energy. But the Should Monster and other negative forces are a part of life that we must learn to manage in order to maintain our positive power. In the following chapters I'll delve into the "how-tos" of protecting and maintaining your positive energy: how to identify and filter out the Should Monster and other harmful forces in your life, and how to avoid, redirect, or let go of low-vibrational forces to protect your high-vibrational state.

Nashville Neighborhood

CHAPTER 28

Recognizing Energy Forces in Everyday Life

If you want to find the secrets of the universe, think in terms of energy, frequency, and vibration.

– NIKOLA TESLA

To maintain the positive effects of unconditional love and other high-vibrational practices, we must know how to mitigate the inevitable energy-draining forces and how to cultivate and grow the energy-charging forces. Recognizing energetic subtleties takes practice and will improve with time and mindful attention. To start recognizing positive and negative energy dynamics, which will help improve your ability to practice belief in love, consider an analogy in the easily understood physical world.

I often receive the question of how to tell when a force is helpful or from the Should Monster, especially when it comes from a source we love and trust. Physical attacks and energetic attacks are both destructive. But while a physical attack may be easily observed, an energetic attack deals with complex emotional and intuitive perceptions, so it may be felt but not initially seen or easily recognized. Over time, allowing too much energetic dissonance (pressure) creates burnout, anxiety, illness, or a number of other physical manifestations.

In the physical realm, someone may have a weapon, be overtly agitated or aggressive towards you, or have invaded your physical space, threatening your safety. Any of those aggressions would be easy to recognize and incite a fight-or-flight defense.

Now consider that an energetic attack may have an equally detrimental impact, yet it is much more difficult to recognize. You've probably heard the saying, "We hurt the ones we love most." Unfortunately, there is truth in that. The most powerful energetic attacks can come from loved ones, trusted sources, and even ourselves. Many of the attacks are reinforced by strong social or religious paradigms, and may be well-intentioned, which make them even more difficult to identify. Increased negative forces attack our positive energy in a number of ways.

One way to identify negative "shoulds" is to be mindful of the forces that are causing negative feelings, such as stress, low self-esteem, frustration, sadness, or anxiety. Exercising this power to scrutinize how certain energetic forces *make us feel* helps us identify and filter out the Should Monster. For example, have you ever felt drained when around a friend who is always complaining? Do you feel like certain topics from a well-intentioned family member suck the life out of you? Those are natural reactions to negative energy (lower vibrations). What you're feeling is the release of your positive energy (higher vibration) to fill the gap energetically. It's a very real signal from your intuition that the Should Monster is near. I liken this effect to the impact experienced through the Second Law of Thermodynamics: *As pressure is applied to a system, it becomes more disorderly and releases heat energy, so it becomes colder.*

Let's use water as a way to visualize feeling frozen in fear energetically by the Should Monster's pressure. Assume our normal operating state is as water, then suddenly we are surrounded on all sides by much colder conditions. If we don't protect ourselves, eventually we will stop moving, turning into ice. Remember, Einstein asserted that "Energy cannot be created or destroyed; it can only be changed from one form to another"— the negative pressures we experience create a force that is literally changing the form of our positive state. It's like those times when we literally cannot get into action when we feel overwhelmed by change.

In my case, I spent a lot of energy trying to help raise awareness and provide solutions for cleaner air and water. Despite the exponential growth of asthma, cancer, and even type 2 diabetes that were all linked directly to man-made pollution, there was, and still is, a lot of negativity around environmental protection. If people don't understand how something is relevant to them specifically, or if the problem seems too insurmountable, they won't get into action. While no one specific encounter caused burnout, over many years, it was like the Chinese water torture mentioned earlier, where drop after drop, over a long period of time, added up to excruciating frustration.

Despite evidence to the contrary, science-backed concerns about our destructive impact on the natural world (not to mention our own health) were constantly shot down as political fiction, hidden agendas, or economically infeasible. That steady drip, drip, drip of negative pressure gradually drained my positive energy sources on the topic. Unfortunately, I didn't have a way to recognize it and filter it at the time. I just kept on, taking the hits and absorbing them like a boxer in the last round of the match who just tries to stay on his feet, getting bludgeoned until the bell rings. I didn't acknowledge the exhausting impact of those energetic punches. Had I recognized them and shielded appropriately, burnout could have been avoided or at least minimized.

I'm not advocating giving up. It's critical to be stubbornly optimistic if you want to incite change in the world. I am suggesting that the "shoulds" of corporate culture traditionally reward us for fighting through obstacles rather than taking time to pause and think about their emotional impact, leading to burnout. While many modern companies have flexible hours, work-from-home options, meditation rooms, and encourage exercise breaks, think of the many corporate cultures where employees are rewarded for having a poor work-life balance. They receive badges of honor for working endless late nights and weekends, without a single accolade for being able to reduce workloads or bring stability to the organization. Words of praise and increased workloads are heaped upon employees, while little support (via improved systems or additional staff) may be given. Cultures wherein leadership opines about having too much work themselves but do nothing to improve balance, set up the perfect environment for burnout because the behavior they are modeling demonstrates that *being miserably overworked is what leaders do.*

As change agents, we must almost always expect resistance to new ideas because the vast majority of people don't like taking new risks or changing habits. Dealing with duties, personalities, or cultures that are not aligned with our own preferences for too long creates burnout. There are tools, such as the AEM-Cube offered by Human Insight, referenced earlier, that companies or individuals may use to identify when there is a lack of alignment or balance in a given role, team, or organization. For example, my results show I prefer getting into action doing activities found at the very beginning of the growth curve, meaning I am energized by inciting new ideas. Being aware of that preference reminds me that when I start feeling burned out—like when working in an extremely change-resistant culture or on topics that must remain methodical for long periods of time—to take a step back and recharge (like our proverbial boxer who would stop to refresh upon hearing the bell signaling an end to each round).

It goes beyond work life and into personal life, as well. Being aware that I find change exciting helps me realize the feeling of being drained by hanging out too much with someone who is completely the opposite— who needs to constantly find reasons why *not* to try something new. Once we are *aware* of the energetic differences, it's easy to depersonalize the impact we're experiencing and value the opposing view as a complement to our energetic strengths. Most importantly, we must understand that every person's preference for getting into action is different and equally valuable. Teams or married couples without risk-averse members may overspend, overpromise, and think short-term. Teams or couples without risk takers may look to the past for solutions and struggle with innovation. These aspects of risk aversion and risk-taking occur within every individual as well, so success is about finding the right energetic balance within ourselves and in our interaction with others.

Consider another aspect of the Second Law of Thermodynamics: *A disordered system cannot get back into its original state, but the molecules released during change may form into something more orderly with newly found energy.* This happened in my neighborhood recently. In the midst of disaster, chaos and disorder transformed into incredible beauty. Here's how it happened:

The Transformation

I live in a neighborhood of downtown Nashville. Just to the east a beautiful Greenway winds along the mighty Cumberland River; a few blocks to the west stately Greek architecture and green spaces offer views of the Capitol at the historic Bicentennial Mall Park; and nearby to the south, flashing neon lights and jangling country music flicker and vibrate through the famous honky-tonk strip. It is a perfect area for an empty nester with a seemingly endless supply of nearby restaurants, friendly neighbors, and lots to do. Another thing I love about the area is avoiding the gridlock of traffic on morning commutes.

I'd only been in that location about six months by March 3rd of 2020. I was abruptly awakened in the middle of the night to what sounded like a rumbling freight train right outside my window and it was growing ever closer, ever louder. First, I thought it was a wild dream after having two margaritas at my favorite Mexican restaurant just before crawling into bed a few hours prior. The windows shook and made crackling sounds along the edges, and my ears popped inside as if I were in the belly of an aircraft ascending into the clouds. The sky was an eerie color even though only the moon was out. The blinds rattled while the windows remained locked shut.

Think, dammit. Think. Breathe. The power is out. Flashlight? Use the phone's flashlight. I yanked the phone off its charger so hard the plug flew out of its electrical socket and slid across the wooden floor. *Get away from these windows—oh gosh, oh gosh, they're going to shatter. Clothes!!! Where the hell are some freakin' clothes?! Hurry! Oh God, dear God, please don't let the windows smash in until I have clothes on ... Where do people in high-rise buildings go during tornados? Stairwell. Get to a stairwell. Go! Shoes? You don't have time for shoes.* **Just run!!** As I rounded the sofa in a sprint for the front door it hit me. Silence. Deafening silence.

It all happened so fast. Within moments, the loud roar of tornado sirens and emergency vehicles filled the air. I gingerly stammered out onto the balcony, as did many other confused neighbors. The courtyard parking lot was littered with uprooted signs, sheet metal from the baseball stadium down the block, trash cans, and other debris I couldn't identify in the dark of night. I was numb. Ears still ringing and not logically thinking, I dialed my friend Gustavo, who lived in the condos across the street. I guess I wanted someone to tell me they had just experienced the same thing and that we were all OK and that it was all going to be fine.

"Hola, mi amiga!" he said, sounding unfazed.

"Are you OK? What happened?" I felt the blood pumping and heard the rapid beating of my heart above the whirring mayhem of alarms sounding outside.

As if an angel had whispered into Gustavo's ear to let him know exactly what I needed to hear in that moment, he kindly and calmly said, "I'm fine, Tab. It's OK, kid. We had a tornado touch down. The power is out, but you'll be OK until morning. Go back to sleep. You're just fine." I thanked him and returned to bed where my mind raced. I wanted to go outside and walk around the streets to see why so many police cars were outside the buildings. I wanted to turn on the TV or search for information on my phone, but only had one bar of service and no Wi-Fi. The storm must have taken out the cell towers. I'm glad I had enough connectivity for the call to Gustavo.

I double-checked the alarm on my iPhone. Still set for 5:30 a.m., *four hours from now,* I thought. I closed all the unnecessary apps to preserve its remaining battery life until then. I had been looking forward to leading a large training session of nearly 100 team members for a Fortune 400 company that day. It had taken a lot of preparation and with that many people taking time for a two-hour workshop, and nobody else working alongside me, not showing up wasn't a feasible option. There was no way I was going to sleep. I decided after a couple of hours to get together my business clothes and drive the 15 miles south to the Brentwood-based office building. It had a gym with a shower where I'd at least be able to get ready for the day with hot water and have electricity to make coffee. And, I could get the news to find out what happened.

Hoping I'd grabbed all the necessities, I got in my car and pulled up to the garage door, realizing it wouldn't open without power. I got out and pulled the emergency-exit belt on the side of the giant garage door and heaved it upwards to get out. Driving out of the building's corridor was like being in a video game of obstacles—there was part of a balcony, a chair, downed power lines, glass, insulation ripped from buildings that no longer existed, and the collection of oddities I'd seen from my balcony earlier. It was like a war zone. The police had already blockaded the entire section of streets, starting at mine. I explained that I needed to get out to go to work and would be heading south, away from the hardest hit area. The policeman grimaced, "Listen lady, I don't think anybody is going to work today. Have a look around for God's sake." Then, he reluctantly let me pass.

All morning leading up to the workshop, I thought to myself how much I appreciated the team members at that particular company. They worked in technology and were used to being startled awake in the middle of the night to fix things. Sometimes, they worked days on end until solutions could be implemented, and they never complained. I stood in front of their managers in my mind and thought about all the things I wanted to say to them—that I had a new appreciation for their lack of sleep, that I was in awe at how they could lead through one frenetic problem after another, and that I had experienced something tragic just hours before so I wouldn't be my usual silly self.

The day progressed and I didn't mention the tornadoes for fear of allowing emotion to catch up with me. Upon reaching the podium that morning, I went numbly into cruise control and said nothing of the things running through my mind. I even forgot to introduce myself or establish the context of my background, jumping straight away into the materials without the usual humor and enthusiasm. But it was what I could muster in the moment. It's not that people wouldn't have been receptive; I just knew if I started to get choked up, I wouldn't be able to get them through all the activities planned during the workshop.

We later learned 24 people died in Tennessee that horrible night. Power and Wi-Fi were unpredictable for weeks until the infrastructure could be repaired. Thousands in my area had been displaced by the mighty storm and two locals were killed. Within eight days after the tornado, the coronavirus was declared a pandemic and the systemic lockdown process began. It was a lot all at once.

My only family lived out of state, but in times like these, your neighbors and friends become your family. How was all this impacting us energetically? Back to that Second Law of Thermodynamics: *A disordered system cannot get back into its original state, but the molecules released during change may form into something more orderly with newly found energy.* Things would never be the same in our neighborhood. Massive apartment buildings had been condemned indefinitely. Initially they were too unsafe to enter to retrieve belongings, then the mandatory Covid-19 containment restricted workers and volunteers from cleaning up. Restaurants were leveled, businesses reduced to heaps of insulation and scattered bricks, telephone poles snapped like toothpicks, and frayed electrical wires dangled about.

But amid all of this disorder, we still had the choice of what to do with the swirling, confused, undirected energy from the fallout. And something beautiful happened.

During the days before coronavirus confinement began, strangers helped strangers. Food was shared. Debris was lifted as people walked to and from the local grocery store. Homes were opened to the newly homeless. Temporary shelters sprang up. In addition to local residents, volunteers showed up from neighboring cities and states. We were finding ways to turn part of the energy produced by the tornadoes into positive action.

In the coming weeks, my new self, the one attuned to our ontological energetic state, was highly aware of the energetic drain from chaos, fear, and uncertainty all around us. Everyone felt the unseen negative energy, but few could explain it. I posted a blog about the unseen forces during troubling times using the concepts laid out in this book. As people grappled with the reality of "social distancing" and quarantining in isolation, it was time, more than ever before, to help others understand what was happening to their energy and how to manage it to stay balanced and positive, so they could remain in a higher vibration—connected to the Spirit, self, and love.

Mangroves of the Rio Nandamojo near Junquillal, Guanacaste

CHAPTER 29

Ditching the Should Monster

The only devils in the world are those running in our own hearts.
That is where the battle should be fought.

– MAHATMA GANDHI

Understanding the dynamics between the "should" energy forces and our own energy forces leads to an ability to protect and optimize our own energetic selves. "Shoulds" come in many forms. Some are helpful and meant to benefit us (amplifiers), while others are harmful to our progress and need to be recognized and released (insulators). Since science proves we are entirely energetic beings, and because my experience with electrical energy and behavior change is the perspective from which I draw, my approach is based upon how negative forces impact our energy optimization. They throw us into imbalance energetically, which is difficult to see, but easy to feel. All "shoulds" are based on unique paradigms, shaped by each person's culture, upbringing, experiences, and beliefs.

Consider a strongly opinionated political post on a highly controversial topic that someone has posted on Facebook to observe how people "should" on each other. Many times, those posts solicit equal and opposite reactions. Now consider that the post goes against your personal beliefs and values. The feeling you get upon reading it would be an example of a force that creates a negative imbalance in your energetic state, based upon your unique paradigms and perspective. We naturally want to push back in some way with the other person, or internalize the jab with guilt, anger, frustration, shame, or any number of negative feelings.

Someone else may read the same political post, who holds a different belief system, and the force created would be positive, based on their assigned meaning. The words in the post are neutral. The reader assigns his or her meaning, typically resulting in some impact on their energetic state. We naturally want to do more activities that amplify our energy (produce positive feelings) and less activities that insulate our energy (create negative feelings). Regardless of how we react, there is an energetic cause-and-effect that occurs whether we have control of what we consume (like polarizing social media posts) or not (like the spread of the Covid-19 virus).

This energetic exchange of forces affects our natural optimal state. The forces may be self-imposed, like perfectionism, or external, like requirements for a college degree. They may be positive, accelerating our well-being or happiness, or they may be negative, blocking or pushing against our forward momentum. They may be material, actually occurring during our waking state, or mental, taking forms such as worries or negative self-talk. Regardless of positive or negative *intent*, each input has the cause-and-effect relationship. Just like Newton's Third Law of Motion, there may be an equal and opposite reaction for "shoulds" that don't align with what fuels our personal preferences or goals.

As another example, consider the energetic impact created from the events that galvanized the Black Lives Matter movement, launching cause-and-effect energetic responses in the forms of outrage, sorrow, and protests against the discrimination and injustice endured by the Black community. Equal and opposite defensive reactions occurred, sometimes fueled through bias. Bias is an often hidden, but powerful insulator. It prevents objectivity and meaningful change if not recognized.

This demonstration of the exchange between activism and defensiveness creates an energetic stalemate that can consume the power of both sides. Significant progress will be made when the majority of people are heading in the same direction. When will people finally understand that we're all made equally, born from the exact same energy source? Fortunately, peaceful, common threads among us are beginning to redirect all sides towards a constructive direction. The hard work to dismantle bias and corruption is gaining momentum.

Unifying energetic forces could help get us moving in a positive direction, like Newton's Second Law of Motion. Amplifiers, those things that accelerate us towards the achievement of our goals, would be examples of positive "shoulds" that serve as catalysts for change or add velocity with encouragement, positive self-talk, guidance, protection, and support. It's up to us to recognize the difference and use the forces to increase velocity in our lives, ignite our passions, and amplify our joy.

If only it could be that simple! Nobody would have to feel stress, anxiety, powerlessness, or burnout. By recognizing the forces—just as I mentioned with the negative vibes of fear, uncertainty, and anxiety with the tornado and subsequent pandemic—we can protect ourselves from the energetic drain caused by those around us and ourselves. The following is intended as a guide to help recognize positive and negative "should" forces.

Positive Shoulds

Positive forces are those things that make you feel energized, bring a smile to your face, or help you move towards a personal desire. When we "tune in to" these positive vibes, it raises our energetic frequency, typically resulting in a feeling like a sense of connectedness, gratitude, or confidence. We often refer to these positive forces in energetic terms. "What he said really resonates with me." "We were perfectly in sync." "Her suggestion accelerated my progress." "She brings a positive vibe to the department." "Your words lit up my day." And so on.

Some "shoulds" can help accelerate you towards positive outcomes like being offered tips that you *should* use to prepare for a successful year-end review at work; being invited by your friend to join her at the gym because you *should* get moving on your mutual resolutions; or telling yourself you *should* set aside time to paint or play music on Friday afternoons. More obvious positive shoulds include that we *should* drive on the appropriate side of the road and obey traffic signals.

You can recognize positive "shoulds," whether from internal or external sources, because they get us moving, amplify our happiness, add velocity to our goals, keep us safe or healthy, and brighten our mood. While it may not be instant gratification, they will sustain or raise our vibrational energy over time. When this happens, we feel good, or at least better than our previous state. High-vibration emotions are things like love, faith, happiness, and joy.

Optimizing our personal energy is what keeps us healthy, connected, and fulfilled. But it is important to note: Optimization of our personal energy requires maintaining a mindful balance between participating in activities or thoughts that require increased energy output versus those that recharge us. Exerting too much personal energy, without recharging, leads to inefficiency and burnout.

It's easy to understand this dynamic when thinking about our physical homes. Imagine the electricity has gone off in your neighborhood and it's freezing cold outside. You decide to build a giant bonfire in the middle of your living room. The blaze is beautiful, it keeps you warm, and everyone roasts marshmallows. Short-term, the positive benefits feel good.

After a while, what seemed like a good idea at first begins to have negative consequences. There's no system in place to channel the heat elsewhere in the house, so the bedrooms are freezing cold. The house wasn't designed to have a fire inside, so without having a vent to allow some of the smoke and heat to escape, it becomes uncomfortably hot in the living room and hard to breathe.

Caution—just because something energizes us initially, it could still end up being an energetic drain. Some can relate to experiencing this type of imbalance by doing too many positive things. We volunteer at our kid's school, we cover for our colleague so he can take vacation, we coach a little league team, we agree to mentor a young professional, and the list goes on and on. Our fires are burning brightly, but perhaps the distribution of our energy gets out of balance and spread too thin—maybe less of it reaches our family, or we are no longer able to generate that spark at work, or perhaps we neglect our own self-care.

A final example of having too much of a good thing is dealing with addictions. A drink, a cigarette, and a giant doughnut all feel great for the instant we consume them. They feel temporarily positive, but in excess, they can drain us of energy or numb us over time, leading to an inability to recharge and raise our vibrational energy. These are just a few situations that represent the complexity of sorting out what will provide an optimal balance over time in our lives.

Negative Shoulds

On the contrary, negative forces make you feel drained, create a sense of imbalance, or distract you from following your personal desires. When we tune in to these negative vibes, it lowers our resonating frequency, typically resulting in an assigned meaning like a sense of isolation, resentment, fear, or doubt. We often refer to these forces in energetic terms like "We aren't even on the same wavelength." "I feel powerless every time I listen to the news." "Her complaining sapped the energy right out of me."

Let's consider the opposite approach to exerting too much positive energy in our example of losing your neighborhood's electricity in freezing-cold conditions. In the darkness and encroaching cold, you held a family meeting, and—due to fear, worry, or doubt—nobody could agree on the best way to provide temporary heat. One parent feared going outside to collect wood in the darkness; the other questioned creating too much toxic smoke in the house. The child feared the dog would get burned, and the dog worried that the goldfish's water would dry up. Allowing too many boundaries from negative energy and being unwilling to take risks means we are stuck in analysis paralysis, are unproductive, and are therefore powerless.

Because they were paralyzed by the thought of taking the risk, they became literally frozen with fear and couldn't get into action. In another scenario, perhaps they tried to mitigate all the risks of building a fire and ended up with so many insulators and protectors designed for the blaze that its heat could not produce enough warmth to survive.

I became out of balance in this way by constantly insulating myself and others from disappointment. I wasn't willing to take the risk of standing my own ground, so I deferred my own needs and wants in service to what others needed and wanted. I mostly did this with personal life when it came to the social paradigms of what an ideal mom and wife "should" be, based on the dominant values within the South. I allowed the inputs of others to snuff out my own instincts to the point where I couldn't even recognize my own desires. My own values had become so insulated and walled off by all the things I *should* do, which was consuming my energy, that I forgot what it was like to follow what I wanted to do, which would have recharged my energy. It's important to have a balance between the consumption and recharging of our energy resources. Becoming attuned expands beyond our mental and behavioral aspects, it also manifests in having a healthier, more energized physical state.

Insulators and risk avoidance are not all bad, of course, and some protect and benefit us greatly, making them positive shoulds. Initially an action may feel restrictive, limiting, or resistant, but sometimes those short-term negatives are vastly outweighed by the long-term balance they bring. For example, requiring a driver's test and agreement to follow traffic rules may seem confining, but driving amongst thousands of others simultaneously requires structure or it could have fatal consequences to ourselves and others.

Filtering Positive and Negative Shoulds

It's not always obvious whether an influence is for our own best interest or to get us to conform to someone else's perspective. Sometimes, we feel compelled to listen and react to pressures, even if they don't align with our values, because we want to please our friends, our families, and even ourselves. Over time, doing things that aren't in sync with our own desires creates burnout. Each instance is like an invisible leech sucking out our power. To help identify these negative forces, the following process may be used to keep us from being "should on."

First, identify whether a "should" is helpful or harmful. Since quantum science has proven we are actually made up of quanta or little packets of vibrating energy, it makes logical sense that our language provides a plethora of clues for whether a force will insulate or amplify our optimal balance (sense of fulfillment). The lists below provide groups of words for which to listen—these words will help you determine whether to receive or filter out advice.

Consider each input, whether internal or external, material or mental. Give yourself the space to think about the impact of each force to your energetic balance *over time*. What may seem like a positive thing at first (e.g., doughnuts, alcohol, recreational drugs, or a one-night stand) may create the risk of imbalance or reduce your power over time. Determine which list best describes the way you feel energetically about a force's impact on your life. It's important to think of any force through the lens of its *sustainable consequence*, not just immediate impact.

POSITIVE SHOULDS *(Support or move us forward)*	NEGATIVE SHOULDS *(May be beneficial or detrimental—take the Should Monster Quiz to find out which)*
I feel...in sync, resonating, spun up with joy, vibrating, lit up, transformed, accelerated, amplified, ignited, positive, tuned in, connected	I feel...isolated, cut off, out of sync, off track, spun up with anger, powerless, insulated, slowed, stopped, inhibited, forced, negative, limited, confined, restricted, frayed, fragmented, out of balance

If forces support sustainable positive results, they do not need to be filtered out. If they inflict negative dissonance, even if they were given with the best of intentions in mind, we may want to put them through a second filter to determine whether to consider the input as sustainably helpful or harmful. If in doubt, use the quiz found in the Workbook section of this book, Recognizing the Should Monster.

Stand Up for Your Authentic Self

It's hard to take the risk of making others unhappy, disappointed, or hurt. Many of us are accommodating pleasers to our own detriment—bending over backwards for everyone else in sacrifice of our own well-being. If you've identified a "Should Monster" in your life, even if it's yourself, I want you to know you are not alone. Don't be afraid to stand up for your own needs, wants, and values, even if they're different from that of others.

Referencing my own experience with being violently attacked during my final year of high school as an example, I allowed the risks of disappointing my friends and family, or even worse, God, to keep me silent. The fear of judgment for "putting myself in a position" to be harmed, the shame of feeling tarnished, and the pride of the image I'd worked hard to build prevented me from taking proper care of myself mentally and physically. At first, the negativity manifested in a silent resentment of others. *How could they complain about seemingly insignificant things, like not getting the prom dress they wanted or who was in the cool kids' clique this week?*

Things that seemed important to my peers seemed ridiculous to me because I had begun closing off emotionally to avoid feeling the pain. Like many, I thought avoidance was a more efficient way of dealing with an uncomfortable situation. Over time, and through enduring decades of men using the Bible in various ways to validate sexual subjugation of women, the resentment and frustration manifested in me pushing away men who tried to get close romantically. I would make up excuses or pick apart trivial things to force a breakup. Eventually, not taking the risk to challenge tradition and seek help for myself led to exhaustion and avoiding emotions altogether.

But what great wisdom has arisen from those tragedies! It may have taken decades to open my heart to the possibility of a romantic interest again, but as long as we're still alive, we may choose to change, to redirect, and to act into positivity. In the U.S., the sad fact is that there are more animal shelters than there are places for victims of domestic violence. Women—and children and men—who suffer from violence, harassment, and other forms of abuse deserve better. I deserved better. I am grateful for the lessons learned, and by sharing them with others, I'm showing it's absolutely OK to take the risk of vulnerability and judgment. What I care about now is helping others avoid decades of unprocessed pain and numbness. If my story can help one person, just one, then taking this gamble is entirely worth it.

If you don't defend your personal energy balance, you'll eventually lose productivity, become anxious, and burn out. It all starts with feeling off-balance and uncomfortable, then builds into exhaustion if not acknowledged and dealt with appropriately. Remember, since we are all energetic beings originating from the same energy, we are all connected, so we naturally have access to the Spirit's energy anytime we need it.

We never have to conform to something that goes against our values, beliefs, or health. We are strong enough to take the chance of accepting our authentic selves. Our *personal definition* of success is what matters. We are powerful and worthy despite what the Should Monster may tell us. That power to be fulfilled, purposeful, loved, and at peace is available to all, if we'll just take the risk to ignite it. I'll even let you borrow a light to get started.

Hanging Bridge in La Fortuna

CHAPTER 30

Defending Against Energetic Attacks

Rage—whether in reaction to social injustice, or to our leaders'
insanity, or to those who threaten or harm us—is a powerful energy
that, with diligent practice, can be transformed into fierce compassion.

— BONNIE MYOTAI TREACE

Defending against the energetic attacks, represented here as the Should Monster, is often not easy, especially when energetic attacks can come from well-intentioned friends, family, or colleagues. The most important aspect of defense is to protect your own positive energy. A relevant energy law to keep in mind when defending yourself energetically is Newton's Third Law of Motion: *For every action, there is an equal and opposite reaction.* As soon as you recognize a negative force coming your way, it's critical to understand that by reacting, you are giving away your own positive energy in the process.

Allowing the loss of too much positive energy, whether it's engaging yourself in negative self-talk or expending effort to combat a negative attack, creates energy imbalance. A series of imbalances, over time, leads to burnout. My energetic description of burnout is when we are no longer able to feel consistently positive energy or are unable to recharge ourselves to a positive state of being. It is so prolific that the World Health Organization classified Burnout as a syndrome in May 2019. Further, according to Pew Research, 7 in 10 U.S. teens rank anxiety and depression higher than bullying, drugs, or gangs, and the youth suicide rate is the highest it has been since 2000.

Since energy is defined in physics as the capacity to do work, being drained of it means we lose our productivity professionally and personally, lacking the sparks of curiosity, inspiration, and self-renewal. The following steps will help you defend against the Should Monster while protecting yourself from burnout.

Disconnect to Protect

One of the best ways to preserve your optimal energy is to not emotionally engage with negative forces, but rather to "disconnect to protect."

If you've stepped foot into a martial arts or self-defense class, the first rule of thumb to mitigate threats is to decide between fight or flight. Flight is always preferred to avoid the risks of injury, with fight being encouraged only if the danger is eminent and you have no other choice but to engage and exert force. Energetically, that means you'll be giving away some of your positive charge to someone or something else.

One of the key reasons our society is exhausted is because the pace of change has accelerated more quickly than our ability to adapt. The rate of technological advancement during the year 2000 will be replicated *every 30 seconds* in 2020. It feels as though there is no time to disconnect and recharge. While now constantly connected in the technological sense, we are more isolated and lonelier than ever before. And the Should Monster lurks in the barrage of ads and messages that tell us we need to look and behave in a certain way. Many ads send these messages in subtle or even subliminal ways that, if you're not actively deconstructing them, you won't catch the message in order to filter it. Even the act of acknowledging a gap between yourself and the world's expectations steals your power in a negative way.

By disconnect to protect, I'm referring to disconnecting from a long-term negative draw on your energy. Imagine you are like a small solar-powered generator that creates just enough power every day to run the lights after dark in your home. It's important to optimize that power, because you generate precisely what is needed each day, then consume it each night.

By allowing friends, family members, colleagues, or online haters to connect to and draw from your personal generator for a short time may not have serious consequences. *So what if you burn the midnight oil working on that project for a few nights together?* But allowing them to drain your power for too long or allowing too many people to connect and use your power simultaneously, will lead to burnout—leaving you in the dark.

Each little battle with the Should Monster is a different size and will draw a different amount of energy from your renewable generator. The best way to protect and optimize your own energy is by disconnecting from the negative forces that leave you feeling drained, overloaded, or that you don't have enough power to support alone. Three techniques to safely disconnect include:

1. Identify and demystify. A popular example of this process is Brené Brown's work on vulnerability, shame, and loneliness. She uses scientific research to identify the source and remove the stigma from otherwise energetically draining fears. For example, in her third book, *Rising Strong* (Penguin, 2012), Brown identifies some of these negative forces as made up.

Conspiracies & Confabulations: The most dangerous stories we make up are the narratives that diminish our inherent worthiness. We must reclaim the truth about our lovability.

Brené helps her readers understand why they feel like they're not enough by identifying the source of those feelings. This demystifies the blame, judgment, and shame that often manifests into the meanings (or stories) we tell ourselves.

From my perspective, identifying why a force or pressure feels off, frustrating, or annoying, can demystify its purpose. Perhaps it feels odd because another person's pressure is out of alignment with our values, needs, or desires. Or perhaps we are telling ourselves an invented story about what the pressure means. For example, Susan recently started working in a new area of the company and one of her early assignments was to collect a quick, but important 10-minute assessment from 20 team members so they could participate in an upcoming leadership development session.

Susan had always prided herself on her ability to communicate effectively, and quickly developed an enthusiastic email that informed the team of this requirement, careful to leave plenty of time for responses. Only two people took the assessment. After sending four more follow-up emails, each one polite, but increasing in urgency, she still only had half of the responses needed. It was already three days past the original deadline for submission and only a week away from the event. Susan told herself that the team didn't have respect for her or maybe they just didn't like her and were trying to make her look bad. Perhaps they wanted the job and were jealous. She grew increasingly frustrated and exhausted with each attempt, beginning to lose sleep worrying about it.

Susan finally shared her frustration at the team's lack of action with her manager, Peggy, who was used to interacting with each of the team members and understood the ways each were most easily moved into action. She pointed out that the remaining team members rarely responded quickly to emails. They were, in fact, trained to focus on incoming trouble tickets and put aside anything that wasn't considered a critical need, so sometimes they may forget or miss emails that did not require immediate action. Peggy suggested a quick in-person follow-up or phone call.

Susan reluctantly followed up in a personal way and within 30 minutes of each request, she received the assessments needed. She identified that the lack of response hadn't been a negative force against her—it was simply a preference for getting into action. Some people were naturally more energized by a personal touch while others preferred not to be distracted personally. Susan's doubt and frustration were direct results of the negative meaning she assigned to the lack of response. Once we practice identifying the Should Monster, then its drain on our power can be avoided. Sometimes identifying and demystifying something is enough to disconnect and protect yourself from it.

2. React as your new self. Using the classic psychological technique of asking how our old self would react to a negative force versus how your new self would react, gives you enough pause to consider long-term consequences. In our context, old self refers to the person who does not realize he or she is assigning their own paradigms to events and who is unaware of the Should Monster's influence. The new self refers to the ideal, actualized person we aspire to become, who is keenly aware of how to identify and shield ourselves from negative forces and seek out positive forces. Reacting as our new selves means we take the time to think through whether it's worth the effort to engage in battle over a request, a remark, a judgment, or if disconnecting (walking away) is a smarter solution to conserve positive, higher vibrational energy.

For example, my old self would never have shared publicly my mystical interactions with animals or dream premonitions for fear of being seen as unprofessional. I gave the Should Monster permission to invent the worry that people wouldn't take me seriously professionally if I shared my spiritual side, so I kept it closely insulated within a small circle of friends and family.

My new self understands I have much greater power by releasing and sharing my higher vibrational experiences with others. It recharges me and those around me, giving them permission to share openly in return. My new self chooses to disconnect from cynical sneers to preserve this power I gain from sharing my experiences with others. Taking the time to consider which scenario generates or preserves the most power allows us to make choices that better balance and optimize our energy.

3. Step aside. Ever witness a boxing match when one opponent is swinging wildly at the other, but he keeps moving out of the way and avoiding the punches? We can do the same energetically. This doesn't mean we leave the ring of the battle; it doesn't mean we're ignoring the very real risks, but it does mean we have avoided some painful blows by ducking out of harm's way.

Ester (Abraham) Hicks, who is a best-selling author and thought leader for her work on the Law of Attraction principles, often uses the analogy of "letting go of the oars." She teaches that fighting against the forces acting upon us is like paddling a canoe upstream. The more forces that abound, especially those we cannot control, the more energy it takes to maintain a position or make progress. Hicks stresses the important regenerating act of releasing the oars to flow where energy takes us—consciously choosing to let go.

It's important to note that disconnecting to protect yourself does not mean to ignore a threat. It's important to acknowledge each threat, then filter how best to deal with it. Using my old self story as an example, I spent a good deal of effort both running from and not acknowledging the Should Monster in action. I felt acknowledging the negative energy-sapping forces working against me would distract from my already stretched-thin pace. *How many parents or loved ones battle valiantly for others, but not for themselves?* Inevitably, it leads to burnout. That faulty coping strategy would be like turning on the bathwater, plugging the drain, then leaving the room and pretending the water had stopped without taking action to reduce the flow or turn it off. Eventually, the tub would overflow and create a mess.

A more effective, new-self strategy would be to acknowledge each event that drains energy from us and pause to consider which ones to allow plugging into our generators. This would allow us to slow the flow of water into the proverbial bathtub or at least plan what time to re-enter the bathroom to be sure it had not reached capacity.

Defend Yourself with a Shield, Not a Barricade

Sometimes it is worth taking the risk to rumble with the Should Monster. Before discussing defense strategy, plan to show up with a shield, not a barricade. Barricades are built up to keep things out. I built a high barricade around my heart after some bad experiences in early adulthood. That wasn't an effective energetic strategy because it kept everyone else from getting in and simultaneously kept my own love trapped inside, unable to get out. Barricades are effective insulators from negativity, but they also prevent two-way interaction, so they equally insulate from positivity.

Shields are designed to protect from attack. A person who wields a shield implies he or she is prepared to defend themselves. Shields may be raised or lowered and easily carried along as you move through the world. Your shield can be set aside when you reach a place of safety. It is important to note that people can be spiritual, open, and loving, and also powerfully capable of defending themselves. Here are a number of effective counter maneuvers to help protect your positive energy.

1. Use an invisible shield. Imagine an invisible shield surrounding yourself. The chaos, anxiety, and pressures from energetic threats charge forward and slip around you on all sides, so you remain protected from harm. Consider the amorphous sense of terror that has come with the advent of the coronavirus and the widespread apprehension and negativity it brings. While being aware the virus exists as a threat, imagining an invisible shield to protect from the chaotic vibe around us can help prevent loss of positive energy and productivity. And remember, *belief* is a powerful driver of physical health, so strong, positive visualization only provides upside potential.

2. Try Judo. Another Japanese fighting technique, Judo, meaning "the gentle way," emphasizes winning in combat by using your opponent's weight and strength as weapons against him or her, while preserving your own mental and physical energy. It embodies the principle that mindful technique wins out over sheer force.

My favorite way to use the Judo technique in personal or professional settings is to ask the bully for a suggestion. Haters thrive on getting others to join them in their lower vibrational (negative) state, so don't give them the satisfaction. Calmly acknowledge their remarks, then ask them for their ideas for a more positive outcome. Or ask them to describe what success looks like. It redirects their momentum away from you and back towards them, and you'll likely get one of two results:

1. A brief respite to break the tension and give you a chance to determine your next move, or
2. The person may actually identify a better way of doing things, helping everyone.

Regardless of the outcome, you have momentarily neutralized the negativity.

For example, a neighbor once complained on social media that I *should* feel awful because I was unable to attend the school's field trip to the state capitol as a chaperone due to an important work commitment. Of course, the remark hurt and made me quite angry. It was bad enough to say that, especially since I hadn't committed to attending and my son had very low interest in the trip, but posting it online for the world to judge was an obnoxious and obvious Should Monster move. Instead of hitting back, I leveraged a Judo technique. My response: *Thank you for your concern about my son's well-being. It's important we work together to support each other so our kids have meaningful experiences. Do you have some recommendations for more effectively covering work responsibilities in order to attend the next school event? Your help is much appreciated!*

Her response: *Maybe we could form a Facebook group of classroom parents and take turns covering school events. I'll get started on a page next week.*

By leveraging her desire to take action, but maneuvering myself out of the way, her momentum continued but changed directions. The movement shifted to a positive, rather than negative vibe. What comes to mind from my experience working with electricity is an analogy to transformers. A transformer is a passive electrical device that transfers electrical energy from one electrical circuit to another, or multiple circuits. Energetically, your redirection can focus the energy of your attacker onto a completely different circuit. Or euphemistically, it's akin to what we'd call in the American South "killing them with kindness."

On the other hand, if I had engaged in a social media face-off with the neighbor, it would have required me to expend energy in a direction that would most likely have been met with equal and opposite resistance—thus canceling out my energy. We may observe this dynamic among business and political leaders frequently. For example, Indira Gandhi, the first female Prime Minister of India, encouraged dialogue among different parties, saying, "You cannot shake hands with a clenched fist."

The next time someone is attacking your ideas or actions, try asking a "Judo-style" question. It still allows you to keep your power, but it redirects theirs, and opens up the possibility for partnership.

3. Say "No." Sometimes the hardest action is to risk saying "No." We want others to be pleased, so we take on too much or agree to do things that go against our best self. Sprinkled heavily along the path that led to my personal burnout was one major weakness: I did a lousy job of saying "No" to things that didn't align with my own values and desires. It was easier and took less time to just do whatever it took to keep the peace and the pace.

Practice saying "No" in a way you're comfortable with, such as, "I appreciate your concern, but that is not aligned with where I'm heading right now." Or, "I wish I had the time to give that project the type of commitment it deserves, but I just don't right now." The more you practice saying it, the more liberating it becomes!

We have to build an infrastructure within ourselves that allows us to connect to the wisdom of intuition—one in which we filter out unhelpful "shoulds"; practice the mental-ninja-like art of protecting and growing our high-vibrational energy; believe in the Spirit, self, and love; and take actions that are rooted in our unique purpose. I learned while watching the Netflix series "The Mind Explained" that Mexico City actually gets more rain annually than London. Even though the life-giving water in their metropolis is more abundant, Mexico City has not set up its infrastructure to make use of it, so it rolls off without providing the sustenance needed, resulting in drought-like conditions.

When protecting your own life-giving energy resources, be intentional about building an internal infrastructure that allows you to drink in and protect the wisdom of intuition—it takes time and planning but will increase your spiritual nourishment and fulfillment.

Remind Yourself You are Loved and Not Alone

The feeling of isolation during the coronavirus pandemic's mandatory containment spread as rapidly as the Covid-19 virus itself. According to census data, over 36 million Americans live alone. Before containment, those living alone interacted freely with others. During the period of forced shelter-in-place orders, however, the full impact of isolation was felt—and exaggerated by the stressors of the health scare, access to food (and toilet paper), and unemployment risks. An article by Robin Wright in *The New Yorker* cites expert opinion that the risks of depression and the type of Post-Traumatic Stress Disorder (PTSD) associated with war or natural disaster events could likely be even higher with the coronavirus pandemic because there is no definitive end date. Further, trauma is compounded because people are not getting the same chemical releases that come from human-to-human contact, leading to short- and long-term health consequences.

While we are physically alone, and most recently alone against our personal preference, we are never spiritually alone. There is an endless supply of renewable power and love available to all who wish to tune in to it, as discussed in the "Believe in Self" section. I strongly believe every living thing is unconditionally loved. Even if we're not feeling connected or loved by others, we can still tap into the love of the Spirit and we can practice loving ourselves by doing the things that bring us joy.

Remember, you're not the only one feeling lonely or isolated—a huge number across the globe share this same pain. It has been inspiring to witness the myriad of ways people have shown connectivity to help reduce the severity of forced containment and isolation. Signs of hope have been placed in exterior-facing windows, online social meetups and Zoom meetings are going on at all hours, volunteers are making grocery runs for immunocompromised strangers, community members are buying restaurant vouchers to help local eateries bridge the gap financially, and calls and letters to loved ones grew just as the spring flowers returned—all bringing much-needed acknowledgement of the energizing and life-affirming truth: You are loved and are not alone.

Riding Spirit on Cliff in Guiones

CHAPTER 31

Recharging and Maintaining Optimal Energy Balance

Your personal vibration or energy state is a blend of the contracted or expanded frequencies of your body, emotions, and thoughts at any given moment. The more you allow your soul to shine through you, the higher your personal vibration will be.

— PENNEY PEIRCE

Once we have connected to our intuition and learned to filter out negative energy forces, we must take care to recharge and maintain our optimal energy balance. While we are accustomed in Western societies to think of fuel as something external—such as gasoline for an automobile, batteries for a flashlight, or the charger for our mobile devices—in the context of this book, power comes from within. Spiritual recharging is the act of recognizing high-vibrational activities, like love, happiness, and compassion, then finding ways to do them more often to maintain the frequency. Setting in place an optimized, high-vibrational balance between yin and yang is key to sustained happiness.

Last year I served as a running guide for athletes as part of Achilles International. One of my favorite partners was Theresa. A highly intelligent achiever, she excelled both socially and academically, studying engineering as one of few females in that field in the 1980s. She lost her vision unexpectedly as an adult. The doctors were uncertain why, but thought it was a result of an infection that grew too quickly to reverse the damages. I used my physical sight to provide guidance, while she provided me with her own form of direction by sharing her unique wisdom, perspectives, and friendship.

It was incredibly inspiring to witness her complete trust in me by running along holding on to only my elbow as we navigated along busy city streets, pet-filled greenway paths, and crowded races. It helped me increase my own trust in others. If Theresa was unavailable, I would be paired in a similar way, with someone else who had their own special gift to share. Each time I volunteered, high-frequency, positive vibrations charged up my energy, allowing me to reconnect with joy, fulfillment, and happiness. Maintaining that higher frequency came with the practice of repeating the same behavior over a period of weeks. The key to happiness is sourcing what recharges you in your own unique way and then doing more of it over time.

It's easy to get lost in a world of feeling "not enough," but these tips can help anyone recharge with positivity. The three techniques below can help you feel revived and protected.

1. Choose something in your life for which to be grateful and focus on that feeling. Our brains are naturally wired to remember negative occurrences because from an evolutionary standpoint, it helps us reduce risk and protect ourselves (like remembering the sound of a rattlesnake). When the mind is completely occupied in gratitude, however, it cannot simultaneously feel fear, insecurity, or burnout. This conscious shift to gratitude helps rewire our outlook and recharge personal energy.

A simple habit-forming technique is to keep a small journal at your bedside and encourage other family members to do the same. Challenge yourselves to pen three things for which you are grateful every day. Whether it's in the morning, to set your tone for the day, or at bedtime, to help ease your mind into a more relaxed state, it's an easy habit to begin that will have immediate positive effects. (The Workbook section of this book provides space to practice your first week of gratitude journaling.)

2. Believe that you can affect your own life in a positive way. As noted earlier in this book, research shows our positive beliefs alone can recreate the effects of drugs, reduce pain, improve relationships, and boost overall well-being. Speakers like Tony Robbins make millions by sharing techniques to help people set their personal vision and practice belief in obtaining it. Quantum cognition also reinforces the assertion that our personal observations and behaviors shape the world around us.

In short, focus your energy in the belief that you are making a difference, healing others, and accomplishing positive things. What is your personal power mantra? What is that thing you'd like to accomplish today, this week, this month, and this year? How do those goals align with your life game? Take a moment to write them down in your bedside journal (or in the Workbook section) and then practice *believing* that they will occur. The act of writing them and consciously visualizing and feeling that those goals are coming true greatly increases the likelihood of them turning into action.

3. Take time for biofield balancing, prayer, or other spiritual practices. They are proven to significantly improve physical and mental well-being. Each of these practices is rooted in the simple, abundant, and endless supply of universal energy. Just as the physical and mental practice of yoga prepares our receptivity, practicing energetic balance, focus, and connection nudges us closer to enlightenment and helps us sustain it. The source of this Light is referenced in many religions and traditions dating back to the origins of mankind. It is available 24 hours a day, seven days a week—we just have to tap into it.

It's natural to feel off-balance with fear, uncertainty, and energetic drains all around us, but don't forget about the unseen impact it is having on your energy and well-being. Remember to protect yourself, redirect your energy into a high-vibrational realm, and recharge. The simple act of stepping into a quiet room for a few minutes to take a few deep breaths, imagine a balanced energy flowing throughout your body, and visualize a positive outcome for your next encounter can instantly reset burnout and stress levels.

No two people will achieve their optimal energy balance in exactly the same way. Since our personal energy may seem like an abstract concept or hard to recognize at first, I'll demonstrate a parallel between managing our own power and overseeing the energy in our homes. While it's a simplified analogy, it may help show that optimizing our potential is not so different from how we manage external forms of electricity.

1. Identify what success looks like.

- In-Home Energy: Decide what temperature you want—some like it warmer or cooler depending on personal preferences—but have a goal in mind.

- Personal Energy: Understanding what personally energizes us is critical. If we are jazzed up by working with people, we would not want to lock ourselves into a job with little interaction. If we are excited by creating change, we would not want to be in a role where routine standardization was constantly needed. By identifying where the potential energy of each person lies, we are better able to identify opportunities for peak performance, increased innovation, and avoidance of burnout.

2. What's the surrounding environment like?

- In-Home Energy: It can be 100 degrees outside, below freezing, or fluctuate in between. The systems we design to power homes vary based on the weather geographically. In the Southwest, solar performs great. In the Northeast, natural gas may be better. It's not one size fits all, because the methods we deploy to heat or cool a home depend on the environment around it.

- Personal Energy: What is the environment around you? Is it full of insulators like drugs, stress, or negativity? Or does it have amplifiers like encouragement, creativity, and freedom? Depending on what surrounds us, we either give or receive energy. Being aware of the environment, and adjusting our flow of energy accordingly, is important to maintain an optimal positive state.

3. What are your sources of power?

- In-Home Energy: Are we using finite resources, like coal, or renewable resources, like solar or wind? What are the costs and conveniences of each? How does each impact residents long-term (does it cause pollution, or will it require maintenance in a few years)?

- Personal Energy: Are we doing things to amplify our energy like exercise, healthy diet, engaging in activities that stimulate us, and listening to our intuition? Our renewable source of energy is available at any time. Consider the most effective way that you are able to tune in to your spirituality, and don't feel like you must conform to how others tune in to theirs. There will be advantages and disadvantages to every method of tapping in, so find what works for you to maintain balance over time.

4. What is the maintenance plan?

- In-Home Energy: Maintaining a desired temperature in a home means taking care of the heating and cooling equipment. We need to change the filter in the HVAC, periodically clean out the ductwork, make sure the sun can get to the energy-generating panels, and insulate the airways. Without ongoing maintenance, the system operates below peak performance.

- Personal Energy: Maintaining a desired positive vibration means implementing strong habits that reinforce a wellness lifestyle. Make it easier to find your own version of the Inner Owl and recognize the Should Monster by exercising your mind and body, accessing your spiritual guide frequently, and practicing self-care.

The body is naturally capable of feeling a sense of euphoria when we are in an optimized energetic state. This high does not require drugs, but in our Western culture, it does take practice because we are encouraged from a young age to consider spirituality as fanciful rather than practical. The more we exercise gratitude, positivity, and spiritual practices, the better able we are to keep an optimal energy balance, as well as connection to the Spirit, self, and love. And a better balance manifests into healthier minds and bodies as well as greater contentment.

Affirmation

CHAPTER 32

Be Free

*Macaw: Ancient tribes in tropical areas regarded the macaw
as an exalted solar symbol of heavenly fire for its bold colors,
its preference to nest high above the jungle canopy, and its
commanding voice that is used to connect with others.*

"I've learned that people will forget what you said, people will forget what you did, but people will never forget how you made them feel," Maya Angelou said that. It makes me think of how being around my Grandma Alma made me feel … the fearless speedster, soulful cook, joyful gardener. But it wasn't just her effusive and loving personality, it was something more—her energy. That creative, curious, open-hearted sense of joy radiated out from her little house onto the porch and into the purple irises in the fencerow and the summer gardens we planted and harvested together.

The joy I felt around her gave me the freedom to fantasize about the life I wanted to create. You couldn't see this energy, but you could undeniably feel it. I didn't know it then, but it was a high-vibrational energy that was so pure, steady, and strong, it transformed me, beckoned me to do cartwheels and dream as big as my imagination would allow. I understand now why, as a child, I intuitively identified her as a source of peace and direction. Even then, I knew deep in my being that when she passed away, she was still there in spirit; the energetic connection remained.

Fast-forward through years of furiously paddling my canoe upstream; allowing the Should Monster to control my thoughts and actions, thus silencing my own voice; burying my heart in a barricade of busyness; enduring professional heartbreak, a slow death by a thousand paper cuts; navigating an empty nest, divorce, and escaping cancer ... until my bonfire was but a few glowing embers. Pausing to alight again from my revelations about energy, the insights gleaned set in motion a tectonic shift in my soul.

I was astounded how the sources, characteristics, and science of electricity affirm the inextricable, inspiring, and exciting spiritual connections beyond mere electricity coursing through wires as we know it. Realizing this association expands the life-affirming truth that energy is the source of everything. For me, understanding "the source of everything" in this way—that applied to modern relationships, social pressures, and even unexpected forces, like natural disasters and unexplainable diseases—was critical in comprehending what so many religions and even self-help books were trying to convey. They suggest acknowledgement, forgiveness of self and others, and belief as the keys to a meaningful life and blissful afterlife. Energetically, acknowledgement is recognizing and naming the "shoulds," forgiveness is filtering out the "shoulds" and letting them go, and belief is tapping into the Spirit, self, and love to recharge and sustain joy and fulfillment.

I began a journey inward. Against my logic-based brain, I took a leap of faith to begin to listen to, then trust, my inner voice again. It led me to the jungles of Costa Rica, where I felt far enough away to sit alongside the pain and paradigms of the past. And I learned to identify the negative impact of the Should Monster. I practiced raising my vibrational energy, and I learned how to increase and protect it. I felt the importance of balance and I learned to recharge. And perhaps most importantly, I allowed myself to feel and realized the power in experiencing emotion. Our emotions are a compass showing the way to our needs, to what our inner voice is trying to tell us. Mine wanted me to reconnect to the fundamental belief in the Spirit, belief in self, and belief in love—that same high-flying freedom I felt at Grandma's.

I shed the "shoulds" and began to feel again. I grieved the pain that so many women neatly tuck away in silence. I grieved my buried relationships. I grieved my powerlessness to incite concern about the precious environment that supports us all—as well as my inability to eliminate my sons' physical and emotional pain. I wailed my grief into the canopies and a howler monkey answered with his own cries of validation. I began an ongoing conversation with the Spirit, sometimes aloud, and entered into a next-level conversation with all living things.

Beyond my passion for a more sustainable world, I began to enjoy a connection with nature, animals, and the Spirit so profound that I walked out of those tangled vines of a drought-riddled jungle and into a clarifying cloudburst akin to a personal baptism. I felt a clear and compelling sense of purpose from these unseen realms, a conviction to somehow continue the crusade to protect nature and moreover, to *help others*—to not endure the silencing of their voices, to care for themselves, to shed the "shoulds," to feel, to heal from violence (physical, sexual, and otherwise), to shape, lean into, and expand their own visions.

I discovered the bliss of fluid interaction between inner, outer, and spiritual worlds far away from home, but realized the capability was there my entire life. As a child, it came naturally. It had been buried but was reborn. And it set me free. It is incredibly liberating to realize we were all born free to choose what meaning to assign to every action, force, and reaction in our lives. *You were abused because he is jealous, controlling, and holds gender-biased stereotypes, not because you deserved, asked for, or wanted it. You were called bossy for being decisive at work while he was praised for being a strong leader, but you used the situation as a cue to become a boss somewhere else, rather than feeling you needed to withdraw your assertiveness.* We are not slaves for the world's pleasure—once we acknowledge and embrace our innate connection to the Spirit, we are unconditionally and perpetually free.

This gift, our intuition, is accessible to all, regardless of wealth, formal education, material things, or use of intermediaries. When you feel the urge to ask your neighbor how he's recovering, when you experience an inner nudge to invite the single colleague shyly tucked behind her computer to join your team for happy hour, when you adopt that puppy before he is put down—you are actively hearing and acting upon that all-knowing, still, small voice. We are born explorers and lovers of all things. Despite the world's good intentions, we learn conformity breeds acceptance which can leave our inner voice seemingly inaudible. But, it's *still* there.

You'll bring that reconnected inner voice to life when you take action, when you live boldly into the possibility of complete interconnectedness, and when you are in sync with the vibe of the universe. *Would I have found emotional peace without visiting Costa Rica and facing my fears? Would I have become open to the possibility of romance again without taking the risk to explore it with Stephen? What if the nearly overwhelming fear of exposing my painfully personal vulnerabilities to the world prevented me from writing this book?*

Without action, commitment, and risk, powering our potential stops at theory, hope, and aspiration. That's fine for spectators and dreamers, but not for athletes, leaders, movers, shakers, and those who actively manifest their own destinies.

By the end of my journey, with filters in place, paradigms left in the past, and reborn beliefs fully embraced, I began experiencing joy and fulfillment more consistently than at any time during my life. The world trains us to think something is missing or unachievable. It says we are not attractive enough, fast enough, accepted enough, or strong enough. Yet we are beautiful, balanced, loved, and powerful *beyond our wildest imaginations*.

Just before completing this book, I joined a friend for a hike at Radnor Lake Park near Nashville. My mind drifted back in time, as I realized it had been nearly 3 years since living in the Costa Rican jungle. During that time, I practiced making decisions based on my own values versus the desire to please others. I exercised my spirituality by finding peace and joy amidst the encircling storm of distractions. And, I stopped moving fast-forward long enough to hit pause and embrace a greater balance. As I often do now, I asked the Spirit for confirmation that I was on the right path. *Have I appropriately closed the door on the wrong relationships and opened another to the right ones? Have I chosen the most useful events to share in this book to help others while still maintaining healthy personal boundaries? Please show me a bird so unusual, I would know, without a doubt, that it was a sign, not a coincidence, that I'm on the right path.*

Maybe the universe would send an owl, I thought—still stubborn enough to hypothesize the universe's response and actively seek it out. *Nobody would expect to see an owl in the middle of the day, and it would be unusual enough to provide affirmation.* I didn't say much to my companion during the hike, my focus was on the emerging tree buds, the turtles sunning their long necks atop the logs in the lake, and especially looking for the owl to affirm my direction. At times, I'd stop and take a good look into the treetops. It would be a Great Horned Owl and would give me a strong, affirming, "Hoot!" and only I would know what its presence meant. The owl would be perched and looking lovingly down upon me, like a crescendo ending to my *Trust Your Animal Instincts* journey. But it never came … because the Spirit is anything but predictable.

My companion laughing lovingly at me, teased, "It sure would be a *hoot* if you saw an owl this time of day." I kept the faith. If an unusual bird didn't show up, it would be affirmation of a different kind, and I was OK with that. I would rethink things and make adjustments. One mile turned into two … then three … then we prepared to round the last turn after the fourth mile and were only about 200 meters from the car.

My heart sank a little. I stopped looking into the sky and began to focus on the path right in front of me. I nearly bumped into the hikers coming in the opposite direction as I navigated quickly around the man carrying his giant green pet macaw on his arm. My rapid pace continued for about 50 feet past the man, then it hit me just like each epiphany from the Spirit has. I buckled at the waist for a moment to catch my balance. Elated laughter rang out as goosebumps peppered every inch of my body. My friend laughed along in disbelief. We had no words to describe what had just occurred right before our eyes.

I asked to see an unusual bird if I was on the right track. I needed affirmation that by taking this risk—shedding light on some very dark personal events and explaining the energetic connectedness of all in a way that hasn't been done before—it could help others avoid my mistakes and share in the joys of their own transformations. My mind envisioned an owl, which would have been very odd, but not unheard of, that time of day. Yet the unwavering, awe-inspiring, ever-present Spirit had given me an answer beyond my wildest imagination.

This was Tennessee. What were the chances of seeing an exotic tropical bird on a random hike? Impossible. And yet, the bright lime green, red, and yellow bird passed right beside us. His black beak tapped the owner's cheek occasionally as his giant tail feathers flowed beneath the man's knees.

I'm a student of life. I'm learning that there are no limits. I want you to know with absolute certainty that your life, too, is full of surprises and rich with everyday miracles beyond your wildest dreams. It's time to reconnect, recharge your life, and ignite your personal power. I can't wait to see what happens next!

Irises in Grandma's Fencerow

Workbook

Personal Amplifiers & Insulators

Make a list of amplifiers and insulators that are present in your own life here. Practice maximizing and repeating the amplifiers while minimizing and reducing the insulators. This will improve your optimal energetic balance and help you access your potential power more easily.

 Amplifiers:
Activities or thoughts that raise your energetic vibration, resulting in feelings of happiness, joy, enthusiasm, and positivity. Each technique you identify that elevates your positive vibrations, when practiced habitually, makes it easier to tune into your intuition.

Examples could be things like: meditation (which can include many activities or practices, such as prayer, yoga, art, or being immersed in nature), practicing gratitude, hiking, cycling, spending time with a pet, playing an instrument, or listening to your favorite music.

_____   _____   _____

_____   _____   _____

_____   _____   _____

_____   _____   _____

Insulators:

Activities or thoughts that lower your energetic vibration, resulting in feelings of fatigue, isolation, frustration, depression, anxiety, and burnout. Each technique you identify that inhibits a balanced vibrational state makes it more difficult to tune into your intuition.

Examples could be things like: over-analyzing, alcohol, drugs, food as a distraction, ignoring feelings, bias, commiserating with people who consistently have a negative vibe, and burying ourselves in busyness to avoid something.

——————————— ——————————— ———————————

——————————— ——————————— ———————————

——————————— ——————————— ———————————

——————————— ——————————— ———————————

Quiz: Recognizing the Should Monster

Consider a "should" in your life, whether internal or external, material or mental. Determine which list best describes the way you feel energetically about that force's impact on your life. It's important to think of any force through the lens of its *sustainable consequence*, not just its immediate impact.

POSITIVE SHOULDS *(Support or move us forward)*	NEGATIVE SHOULDS *(May be beneficial or detrimental—take the Should Monster Quiz to find out which)*
I feel…in sync, resonating, spun up with joy, vibrating, lit up, transformed, accelerated, amplified, ignited, positive, tuned in, connected	I feel…isolated, cut off, out of sync, off track, spun up with anger, powerless, insulated, slowed, stopped, inhibited, forced, negative, limited, confined, restricted, frayed, fragmented, out of balance

If the "should" inflicts negative dissonance, even if it was given with the best of intentions in mind, we may want to put it through a second filter to determine whether to consider the input as sustainably helpful or harmful. Use this quiz to determine if you're dealing with the Should Monster.

Answer each of the questions below by choosing "Yes" or "No."

(Yes / No)   Did the advice come from someone whose opinion you respect, like a close friend, family member, or trusted work colleague?

(Yes / No)   Is the input real (e.g., not hearsay or conjecture)?

(Yes / No)   Does it align with your personal beliefs, goals, and values?

(Yes / No)   Will following it offer you benefits like protection, safety, education, health, well-being, or long-term satisfaction?

(Yes / No)   Consider the worst possible outcome if you ignore the input. Are you energized by taking that risk?

Based on the number of "Yes" responses, this guide may help you identify things that are sapping your energy and coming from the Should Monster.

0 Yes Responses: You have come face-to-face with the Should Monster, and it is probably best to filter out this input. Note the least disruptive way to energetically filter it out is to simply ignore this input.

1-2 Yes Responses: Consider filtering out this input or to at least delay getting into action until you've had an extended time to consider its impact in your life. Can't tell how you feel about it? Ask your intuition. I like a method from *Put Your Intuition to Work* by Lynn Robinson that suggests asking yourself if you should do something or not: Flip a coin, with heads meaning "yes, do it" and tails meaning "no, don't do it." When the coin lands on heads (yes), what do you immediately want to do? In the split-second after it lands, do you immediately want to go for the best 2 out of 3 or do you feel energized and want to get moving? If this little exercise leaves you wanting to hold out for another flip, then you're probably dealing with the Should Monster.

3-5 Yes Responses: There's a good chance this input may support or amplify your energy in a positive way. Strongly consider this force before discarding it.

Gratitude Journal

It's always a good time to practice gratitude! Focusing on gratitude helps rewire our outlook and recharge our personal energy. Challenge yourself to write three things you are grateful for every day. Use the space below to get started.

Day 1 Date: _____

I am fully grateful for the following three things today:

_____

_____

_____

Day 2 Date: _____

I am fully grateful for the following three things today:

_____

_____

_____

Day 3 Date: _____

I am fully grateful for the following three things today:

_____

_____

_____

Day 4 Date: _____

I am fully grateful for the following three things today:

_____

_____

_____

Day 5 Date: _____
I am fully grateful for the following three things today:

_____

_____

_____

Day 6 Date: _____
I am fully grateful for the following three things today:

_____

_____

_____

Day 7 Date: _____
I am fully grateful for the following three things today:

_____

_____

_____

Notice the shift in your thinking and emotions as you get into gratitude. Do you feel calmer, more powerful, and happier? Consider making this a daily practice, as it will help you maintain positivity and balance.

Personal Power Mantra, Accomplishments, and Life Game

Writing down our personal power mantra, goals, and current life game helps increase the chances of accomplishing them. Use this space to record your temporary thoughts, and remember they may change at any time based on your situation and guidance.

What is your *personal power mantra*? A power mantra is something you say to yourself to provide motivation or encouragement. It can be anything that reminds you to feel good, like a quote, power phrase, a proverb, or an affirmation. Here are a couple of my favorites:

Take risks: If you win, you will be happy; if you lose, you will be wise.
–SWAMI VIVEKANANDA

I think 99 times and I find nothing. I stop thinking, swim in silence, and the truth comes to me.
–ALBERT EINSTEIN

_____

_____

_____

What is something that would make you feel happy or positive that you would like to accomplish today, this week, this month, and this year? While traditional planning indicates one should start with the long-term end in mind, I'm suggesting you begin with understanding what makes you feel good now, practice recognizing it, then extend it into a mid-term or longer period life-game purpose.

Today: _____

This week: _____

This month: _____

This year: _____

How do the accomplishments you listed align to form your life game? Look for themes within the actions that bring you joy. Your life game will be a mid-term goal, say 1-5 years, that is something you feel passionate about working towards for a period of time. It's called a game because it produces fun, not stress, and there doesn't have to be a definitive end. For example, it could be "volunteer more time to help animals" or "to learn how to swim."

Suggested Reading

Existence of universal Spirit power and value of tapping into it

Chopra, Deepak and Menas Kafatos. *You Are the Universe: Discovering Your Cosmic Self and Why It Matters*. New York City: Harmony Books, 2017.

McTaggart, Lynne. *The Field: The Quest for the Secret Force of the Universe*. New York City: HarperCollins Publishers, 2003.

Nelson-Isaacs, Sky. *Living in Flow: The Science of Synchronicity and How Your Choices Shape Your World*. Berkeley: North Atlantic Books, 2019.

Sadhguru. *Inner Engineering: A Yogi's Guide to Joy*. New York City: Spiegel & Grau, 2016.

Human biofield and energetic healing

Brennan, Barbara Ann. *Hands of Light: A Guide to Healing Through the Human Energy Field*. New York City: Bantam Books, 1987.

Brugh Joy, William. *Joy's Way: A Map for the Transformational Journey*. New York City: Penguin, 1974.

Gerber, Richard, M.D. *Vibrational Medicine: The #1 Handbook of Subtle-Energy Therapies*. Simon & Schuster, 2001.

Being brave and taking risks

Brown, Brené. *Daring Greatly: How the Courage to Be Vulnerable Transforms the Way We Live, Love, Parent, and Lead.* New York City: Penguin, 2012.

Goss, Tracy. *The Last Word on Power.* New York City: Rosetta Books, 2010.

The value of tapping into limitless universal power

Bernstein, Gabrielle. *Super Attractor: Methods for Manifesting a Life Beyond Your Wildest Dreams.* Carlsbad: Hay House, 2019.

Hicks, Esther and Jerry. *The Astonishing Power of Emotions: Let Your Feelings Be Your Guide.* Carlsbad: Hay House, 2008.

ILLUSTRATION AND PHOTO CREDITS

ILLUSTRATIONS BY CHAPTER

Charlotte Cash, Drawings for Chapters 12, 16, 17, 32, Workbook

Ethan Crawford, Charcoal drawing for Chapter 27

Kimberly Ghattas, Design for Chapter 24

Dennis Hogan, Design for Chapter 10, Inner Owl logo, Should Monster logo

Tabitha Scott, Watercolor paintings for Chapters 1, 2, 3, 4, 7, 9, 12, 13, 14, 15, 16, 17, 18, 22, 28, 32, Workbook

PHOTOGRAPHS BY CHAPTER

Wayne Edwards, Chapters 11, 29

James Haussermann, Chapters 21, 23, 26, 30

Rob Nowak, Chapter 31

Tabitha Scott, Chapters 19, 20

About the Author

TABITHA A. SCOTT is an award-winning international advisor, speaker, and author. A thought leader in electrical and human energy, her area of expertise is leveraging principles of modern and ancient energy technologies to accelerate innovation, productivity, and the development of personal potential. She led efforts in creating the world's largest solar-powered community and was recognized for her innovations by the White House.

In addition to earning a BS in Finance, an MBA, and a Masters in Bank Management, Tabitha was credentialed as a Certified Energy Manager through the Association of Energy Engineers, in Blockchain through MIT, and holds numerous certifications in human biofield therapy. A Kentucky native, she lives in Nashville, TN.

Please visit www.Powering-Potential.com to learn more about Tabitha's background and expertise, request an interview or book her as a speaker.

Made in the USA
Monee, IL
10 June 2021